Best
PUB WALKS IN
LINCOLNSHIRE

Tony Whittaker

Published by Sigma Leisure – an imprint of
Sigma Press, 1 South Oak Lane, Wilmslow, Cheshire SK9 6AR, England.

British Library Cataloguing in Publication Data
A CIP record for this book is available from the British Library.

ISBN: 1-85058-408-7

Typesetting and Design by: Sigma Press, Wilmslow, Cheshire.

Cover photograph: The Royal Oak, Little Cawthorpe *(Tony Whittaker)*

Photographs: the author.

Maps: designed by the author and completed by The Agency, Wilmslow.

Printed by: MFP Design & Print

Preface

It is a rare joy these days to walk in unspoilt areas that are not a perpetual challenge or upon another continent. Lincolnshire, known for its wide open spaces and small population, also has its towns to offer variety and a rich history which belies the apparently quiet nature of its people. Remote as it may seem, it has been much fought over, witnessed a religious uprising, and played its part in the industrial revolution.

So this is a voyage of discovery as well as a book of walks, spread out over the whole county. The walks are between four and nine miles in length, and try to give you the feel of the different areas of this county whose 1974 boundaries made it about 40 miles wide and 70 miles long. Almost without exception they start from villages, but are often near to fine towns, industrial towns, seaside towns and small market towns. You will also find that the county isn't all flat; and you may be left with a strong impression that you are walking through an enormous food factory. In such circumstances, the pubs are bound to vary and are all good in their own way.

The route maps and notes should help you enjoy yourselves and, maybe, persuade you to find out more about the area. Most of the walks are easy, and even the few that might be considered moderate are only a little harder in parts. I'm sure that this is a county you could grow to like very much.

Accommodation is best left to the tourist information offices and their booklets, as I have not stayed overnight in all the walking areas (although I have mentioned where the pubs provide bed and breakfast). The addresses of the Tourist Offices are listed under `How to Get There' in the main part of the book.

Acknowledgement

I hope the meanderings I have encouraged you to take will give you many pleasant surprises, and that you will want to come back to a county which seems to make a special effort to help and encourage walkers.

This gives me the opportunity to thank the farmers of the county, who, with the co-operation of a number of local councils, have marked and maintained paths, opened up new areas, created nature reserves and, in some cases, made special new walks. With the exception of some areas in the south of the county, obstructions have been almost non-existent and I hope we have shown our appreciation by respecting their place of work.

I hope readers also have reason to be pleased with the hospitality of the pub landlords.

Tony Whittaker

Contents

About Lincolnshire

The Walks

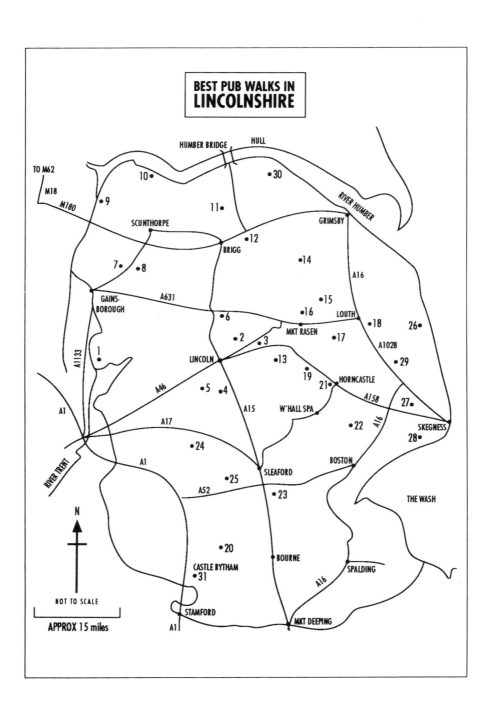

About Lincolnshire

Lincolnshire, like Yorkshire, was divided into three 'Parts' (instead of Ridings) until 1974, when faceless bureaucrats changed the boundaries and the names. I have taken Lincolnshire to mean the area within the pre-1974 boundaries.

Many people think of this area as fenland, daffodil fields or fishing ports. Even when travelling through it, you get the impression that it is a totally placid place. In fact, large tracts have hills as high as most other counties, while the history of the county reveals periods when it obviously played a major part in shaping the future of this country.

The three 'Parts' – Lindsey, Kesteven and Holland – have always been sharply different from one another. Lindsey may once have been an island, bounded as it is now by the Humber, the swamps of Axholme, and the Trent, with shallow meres and the River Witham on its southern border. Kesteven was the forest region (until deforestation in 1230), a continuance of the Lincolnshire Wolds. It went up to the Cliff, the steep slope between Ancaster and Lincoln. Holland is the Part that has changed the most by growing bigger! Drainage schemes, over the centuries, have brought acres of cereal-growing land where previously there was fenland or swamp. This has meant some loss of wild life, including the desperate men hiding from the law and the landless.

That great flat plain of 700 square miles, typified by the great straight lines of its drains and rivers, extends across Lincolnshire to Norfolk and Suffolk and even further inland, to Cambridgeshire. Before the drainage, small farmers existed on narrow strips of land, while monks built great abbeys and made some small scale attempts at drainage. The present man-made landcape only started to appear when Cornelius Vermuyden was brought over at the request of the 4th Earl of Bedford in the 1620s. Without this imaginative Dutch engineer who undertook such massive projects, 200 or even 300 years might have passed before any comparable scheme had been started.

However, the land sprang into life and continued to improve. It has also left us with a network of drains that are difficult to cross and so a good reason to keep our distance as far as pubs combined with walks are concerned. But do not avoid the area altogether: a drive around, probably taking in Spalding, Holbeach and Wisbech, would show you what has been achieved, as well as a few more notable pubs and hotels of note (try the Rose and Crown in the market place at Wisbech, and walk past the rows of fine old Georgian houses). As you would expect, the walks take you through fens, farmland, woods and Wolds, but also near to industrial areas that produce chemicals or road building equipment, ports for fishing boats or oil terminals, plus a fairly generous sprinkling of castles, monastic ruins and historic houses.

Much of the terrain is flat, but it has its two lines of hills, both running more or less north/south. The Wolds, with just three rivers remaining: the Rase, the Bain and the Lud (the others having soaked into the chalk long ago) stretch from the south bank of the Humber towards Woodhall Spa, before appearing to fade out as the layers of chalk prepare to go under the Wash. They vary in width from their narrowest of two or three miles to about 14 miles near the southern end. The other line also starts near the Humber but west of the Wolds and is of a harder rock, limestone. The line has more than one name and although appearing to be very similar, three different sections are called `The Cliff', Lincoln Edge and the Heaths.

The Lindsey marshes in the north east are less protected than the fens from the sea. Lindsey has had its sea defences breached many times over the centuries. These defences are the high and wide natural sand dunes, but they were no match for the gales and heavy seas of 1953. On that occasion, flooding caused the loss of 40 lives and the swamping of over 20,000 acres.

Still in the north east, Grimsby, like Hull, used to claim the biggest deep sea fishing fleet in the British Isles, if not Europe. Now a mere skeleton of the industry rattles along. If you see a side netter or stern trawler on the river or in the docks these days, it will most likely be a survey ship or the base for some expedition, converted for its new job.

Lincoln and Grantham are famous in the engineering world, although Lincoln is a jewel worth visiting for many other reasons. The Romans built their fortress here on a site of natural strength, where the cathedral now stands; and the high ground had been inhabited in the Bronze Age and was also the site of an Iron age settlement. Lincoln was a major port: when the Romans dug their canal, the still used Fosse Dyke, it became the fourth largest port in England.

The south bank of the Humber is the most industrial part of Lincolnshire. Scunthorpe was famous as a smelting town. Boston and Brigg are agricultural centres with interesting markets and the coast has a string of small towns to cater for those who enjoy massive beaches. It is only when the tide comes in over sand that has had at least five hours constant sunshine that I can bear the thought of immersing myself; more often than not, the North Sea has all the charm of a local anaesthetic. Fortunately Cleethorpes and Skegness have other attractions, which, while not likely to rival Monte Carlo, are comparatively cheap and friendly. After all, could Monte Carlo book Ken Dodd two nights a week for the whole season? Incidentally, the county is populated by `Yellow Bellies'. The suggested origins of this name range from field workers who took poppy juices to combat malaria, to the species of frog found in the fens with a yellow underside. Nearer the possible truth is the fact that the Lincolnshire Regiment used yellow `frogs', ornamental fastenings down the front of their uniforms, and the people were proud of their association with the regiment. The same regiment gave the county its anthem, the regimental march `The Lincolnshire Poacher'.

The county is so full of archaeological sites, castles, monastic ruins, churches, chapels, historic houses and gardens, that rather than list them I have confined myself to mentioning those which lie near to the walks. Burghley House, near Stamford, now hosts the Autumn Horse Trials of the British Horse Society and Cadwell Park, besides hosting some very exciting motor bike racing, also holds a one day meeting at the end of August for the Vintage Sports Car Club, when sports and racing cars from the `Golden Era' battle in earnest around a demanding circuit that also has good spectating, and picnicking, points.

How to Get There

As in many rural walking areas, getting there by public transport can be a problem, and bus and train timetables can change dramatically. Lincolnshire has approximately 50 operators who run local bus services, many of them operating only one or two routes in their own locality. The largest company in the area is Roadcar (01522) 532424), which operates services in most parts of Lincolnshire and the surrounding counties. Generally, services along the east coast, particularly around Skegness, do increase in the summer season. But to reach some destinations there is not always a direct service and connections can make the trip fairly lengthy.

Full details of all bus services, National Express and rail services in Lincolnshire can be obtained from the Lincolnshire County Council's Hotline, (01522) 553135, or from its `Bus and Rail Times' booklets. These can be purchased from newsagents and tourist information centres or by post, for a small charge.

All the walks are circular, bringing you back to where you left your vehicle. Regrettably, although the smaller country roads are still very quiet, main roads everywhere are busy, making the car part convenience and part nuisance. Motorbikes may be a slightly masochistic solution, while bicycles are ideal when the sun shines and a gentle holiday of three or four days or more is planned. Should you use the pub car park, please make sure you ask the landlord if you can park there before returning to enjoy his drink or food – or both.

Tourist Offices

The Manor House, West Street, Alford LN13 9DJ. Tel. (01507) 462143

The Guildhall Centre, St Peters Hill, Grantham NG31 6PZ. Tel. (01476) 566444

9 Castle Hill, Lincoln LN1 3AA. Tel. (01522) 529828

Embassy Centre, Grand Parade, Skegness PE25 2UP. Tel. (01754) 764821

The Arts Centre, 37 St Mary's Centre, Stamford PE9 2DL. Tel. (01780) 755611

Walking in the Countryside

Keen and experienced walkers should need no reminding that the countryside is a workplace as well as one of our major food sources. A responsible attitude by walkers will help to preserve the countryside and to maintain good relations beteen walkers, landowners and all those who work there.

What to Take

Common sense, the distance you plan to walk, and the weather will normally help you to decide between a lightweight anorak or quilted stormcoat. If it is cold, make sure what you take is warm, windproof and waterproof. At other times, a pullover (wrapped in a plastic bag) in your haversack might be enough for a four or five mile walk. Lightweight rainproof jacket and trousers become necessary as the walk gets longer and if there is any hint of change in the weather.

For these particular walks, I suggest that you carry drinking water, because of the shortage of shops on most of the walks. I also remain convinced that the ideal footwear for Lincolnshire has to be WELLIES. On a hot dry day I will wear trainers, but even then short wellies are in the car. I prefer to walk in trainers as they are kinder on your feet: walking across farmland usually means mud, which on leather, high-ankled `clompers' starts to make them feel like ton weights. Not only do short wellingtons have a good gripping tread, they can be cleaned easily, even in a puddle, en route.

My final recommendation is to take the appropriate Ordnance Survey 1: 50,000 scale map. Though the walk notes and accompanying sketch map will get you around, the map of the area will show you how the particular walk fits in with local towns, other places of interest, the coast and so on. It could also be useful in an emergency.

Map References

Rather than using the precise Ordnance Survey six-figure map references, as used by experienced walkers, I give the start point of each walk as a four-figure reference – just the same as a road atlas. The two pair of digits give the coordinates of the bottom left-hand corner of the square (on the OS map) in which the starting point is to be found.

Taking Torksey Lock as an example (walk 1), the starting point is referred to as 8378. Get hold of the appropriate OS map (Landranger series; sheet 121) and look at the numbers at the bottom of the map: these are the `eastings'. In this case, find grid line 83. Now look at the numbers that run up the edge of the map (the `northings') and find grid line 78. Find where this grid line crosses your eastings line and that point defines the small square in which Torksey Lock is to be found.

Flora and Fauna in Lincolnshire

Lincolnshire's size and diverse habitats make it impossible to cover the whole county thoroughly, so I have confined myself here to what I have observed in the course of the walks.

Although small pocket editions of books on wild flowers and birds are readily available, I find it more useful to take slightly more comprehensive books and leave them in the car to refer to on my return. My two favourites at the moment are the Hamlyn Guide to Birds of Britain and Europe by Bertel Bruun and The Field Guide to the Plant Life of Britain and Europe, published by Kingfisher.

By the time you have walked a few of the routes suggested in this book, the reason for the differences will become obvious. Wide sweeps of fertile land without hedges as far as the eye can see are unlikely to encourage wild flowers and even the bird life is limited in these parts because of the lack of cover. In the large flat areas of arable land between the the coast and the

Wolds, sea birds may come in to feed. In some parts, Canada Geese are becoming an expensive nuisance: large flocks descend on crops that are two or three inches high, and graze them clean.

The fens have more water fowl, and some dykes are deep enough for part of the sides to avoid sprayed pesticides and weed killers, so that some wild flowers manage to survive. On the hillier ground of the Cliff and the Wolds, there is more woodland, more hedgerows, and a few valleys good for grazing but with sides steep enough to discourage tractors; here you are likely to see more birds and wild flowers.

At the northern end of the Wolds there are more foxes, rabbits, weasels and even badgers, as there is still a good acreage of woodland and permanent or semi-permanent, grazing. Walking through this area is much like that experienced among the chalk hills of any other English county. Defunct chalk quarries are the most likely places to find wild flowers such as cowslips and pink campion. Other shady places may harbour dogs mercury, forget-me-nots and wild thyme. Skylarks and yellow hammers seem to thrive in this area, and it was a pleasant surprise to see orange tip and common blue butterflies as I walked here.

But the star attraction to visitors is Gibraltar Point. Fairly near to the walks starting near Skegness and Wainfleet All Saints, this is one of the most important areas in Europe to observe migratory birds. The red necked grebe and black-headed and herring gulls are common enough for most of the year, but birdwatchers are attracted here by the rarest of Britain's sea birds, the little tern, which nests on the Spit. There are also several pairs of ringed plovers. In autumn, huge flocks of wading birds feed on the mud flats, and herons and kingfishers can be seen from the hides near to the fresh water mere in the Reserve. The Gibraltar Point information centre is well run, offering nature trails, plenty of information and picnic areas. Here you will also find an explanatory display that shows the gradual development of the marshland, as the sea retreats.

The other places I came across that seem worthy of note are widely scattered. Pelham's Pillar, between Caistor and Brocklesby, celebrates the fact that the Earl of Yarborough planted 12.5 million trees thereabouts, before his death in 1823. On the sheep grazing land around Market Rasen, near Linwood, there is a small brown plant with blunt spines, called Iceland moss or bread moss, although it is actually a lichen. It is more common in the Northern wastes and is eaten by Lapps when they have no bread. I still do not know whether I was a victim of the Lincolnshire sense of humour when I was told that it was forbidden to eat it in Britain because of its rarity, and that in any case the plant contains an acid which is harmful to those not used to it.

Linwood is also notable for its trees, one of which, the creeping willow, has been here since soon after the Ice Age, and for its marsh plants. There are still reported sightings of red squirrels. The woodcock, nightjar, butterflies and many lovely moths are more noticeable. If you are near Mablethorpe, you might be rewarded with a sighting of the Natterjack Toad. This increasingly rare species may be found among the dunes five or six miles to the north. It is smaller then the common toad, has a yellow stripe down its back and runs rather than hops.

Previously common birds like the bunting and the skylark are now decreasing in number, but it is unreasonable to blame the farmers who for over 20 years have been encouraged to be as efficient as possible in producing food in Lincolnshire. In the eighteenth century, beef and mutton were the main farm products and game was abundant. After the Enclosures Act at the beginning of the nineteenth century, more grain was grown and efforts were made to reduce wildlife. As in Roman times, root crops continued to be grown but potatoes, sugar beet and, in the Fenland, vegetables increased in acreage considerably. With all this ploughed land, wild deer almost disappeared, although in the southern part of the county (below the A52) muntjak, roe deer and fallow deer are frequently seen. By the mid twentieth century, thousands of miles of hedging had disappeared: you now need keen eyesight and very good hearing to see the wild creatures and flowers that remain.

1. Torksey Lock/Laughterton

Route: Torksey Lock/Laugherton – River Trent – Fossdyke Navigation – Torksey Lock.
A level walk mainly along the banks first of the River Trent and then of a Roman canal.

Distance: 8 miles.

Start: Torksey Lock is the obvious choice with its amenities, but it does get busy and crowded in spring and summer. Laughterton is a good alternative. OS Landranger Series Map 121, square 8378/8375.

Getting there: Torksey Lock is at the junction of the A156 GainsboroughNewark and the A1133. From Lincoln or Worksop, use the A57 and then go northwards on meeting either the A156 or the A1133. Laughterton is 1¼ miles south of Torksey Lock on the A1133.

The White Swan

Situated at Torksey Lock, this is a lovely building for a pub. With only draught Bass, John Smiths bitter and Stones cask to offer, the pub has to rely a lot on its convenience (to the boating fraternity) and on the personality of the landlord and his wife. Food is now available and the pub is open all day 11am – 11pm, including Sunday. Phone: (01427) 718653

The Friendship Inn

At the alternative start point of Laughterton, this pub's opening hours are: Monday – Friday, 11am – 2.30pm, 6 – 11pm; Saturday, 11.30am – 3pm, 6 – 11pm; and Sunday 12am – 3pm and 7 – 10.30pm. Food is served every lunchtime and evening except Sunday evening when live music takes precedence. The beers are Batemans XXXB, Wards, Bass and/or a guest beer. Phone: (01427)718681

Torksey and Laugherton

Torksey was once a major Roman port, and the canal the Romans left behind is probably the oldest man made navigable waterway in England. In the Middle Ages, Torksey possessed a castle, three churches and two religious houses. Only the ruins of the castle are left and the place is a tourist village.

Laughterton is trying to expand a little with an extension of the camping and caravan site into a sports complex of sorts with a small golf course.

Torksey Lock

The Walk

Directions start at Torksey Lock at (A), but can be picked up easily at (E). From the car park at the south side of the bridge over the canal (the car park on the right is free, while the one on the left has a fixed charge – there are other places during midweek), go right and walk along the last bit of the canal before it reaches the River Trent. Here is your introduction to an unusual gate system where two gates of an unusual shape are hung close together, so that one opens towards you and one away from you.

If your walk coincides with a flood tide, I am sure you will be impressed by the speed of the flow and hope, like me, you never fall into this one. As you start the walk along the river bank, the first thing you see is the National Rivers Authority building, which means taking to a path (B) that runs behind it before continuing along the bank (via a rickety old stile) and past the Old Ferry House. There is plenty to see and on this good surface you can maintain a brisk pace if you wish. One day in early spring as I approached the village of Laneham I came across at least a dozen black birds perched in a tree which was in the water at high tide. The birds looked like miniature cormorants so I naturally thought of Shag, especially when a flight of them took off and circled, keeping their heads high with the bill tilted upwards, but

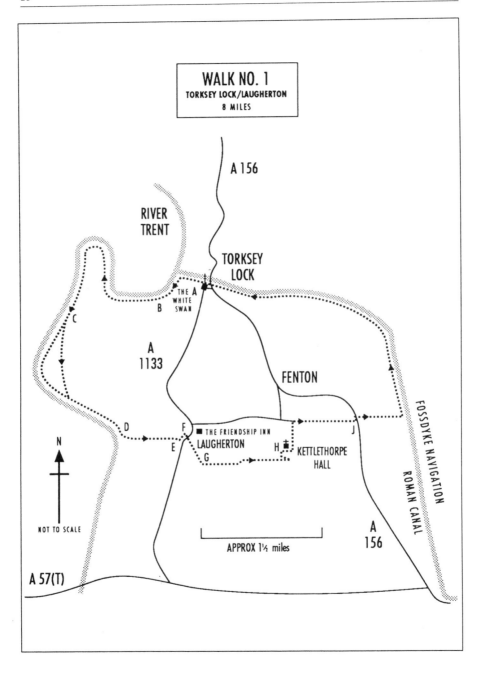

WALK NO. 1
TORKSEY LOCK/LAUGHERTON
8 MILES

A 156

RIVER
TRENT

TORKSEY
LOCK

THE A
WHITE
SWAN
B

C

A
1133

FENTON

N

NOT TO SCALE

D   F
        E   THE FRIENDSHIP INN   J
            LAUGHERTON   H
            G   KETTLETHORPE
                       HALL

APPROX 1½ miles

A
156

FOSSDYKE NAVIGATION
ROMAN CANAL

A 57(T)

these are almost exclusively found near salt water and rocky cliffs; later someone suggested pygmy cormorants (which I had never heard of) but which do prefer rivers and lagoons.

Laneham has two splendid riverside houses with either verandah or balcony overlooking the river. There is a water ski-ing club as well, which is a good excuse to sit and watch for a while.

After that as the river comes from the left, the path moves away from the bank for a while at (C); you rejoin along the straight bit and turn off to the left just as it starts to swing right again (D). A 67-kilometre post warns you of this lane which goes under some power lines and skirts the edge of what was Laughterton Marsh but now, although low lying, is under cultivation. The lane starts to pass houses and shortly after meets the main road through the village. This is (E), your alternative starting point.

Go along to the left, and take the next lane on the right, Sallie Bank Lane(F). Walk through this small housing development, turning left at (G). This lane goes past farm buildings, greenhouses and a cattery before a red brick house on the left, where the path turns left into a field with a hedge on your right-hand side until a metal bridge is visible on the left-hand boundary. Change direction and then cross the bridge.

Just after the bridge cross a smaller bridge over a drain; as the drain or ditch changes direction, the path carries straight on with the ditch running alongside on the right. Heading for the hamlet that can be seen in front may give you time to notice that there are many more molehills than seen before, or elsewhere. Does Lincolnshire have a special attraction that only moles know about?

At the other side of this field is another stile that lets you out onto a farm road. Turn right and walk along it. This will bring you to Kettlethorpe; walk straight ahead with the church on your left to see the hall on your right behind the remains of a gatehouse. Now return along the path, turn right and go through the lych gate (H), walk toward the church and then follow the path to the left. An iron gate on the left which gives access to the field. Head for the end of the gardens of the house ahead and to the left by way of the avenue of trees.

After passing this and other houses the path continues in the next field, now with a post and wire fence on the right. Keep going in the same direction until a green lane crosses your front. Here the path goes to the right until the road is reached at (J). Cross the road and go left for a few yards before turning right down a farm lane.

At the bottom there are a number of sheds, probably disused chicken sheds. Go down the left-hand end between a shed and the gas container. At the other end, walk towards a minor building that stands alone below the bank. Climb the bank and you will see below a stout plank across the ditch. You can either cross here or go left along the edge of the next field to a bridge of more substantial proportions. Either way, the objective is to get onto the next bank, which you will soon see is the bank of the Roman canal an especially straight stretch of two and a half miles, just like their roads.

Once round the bend of the canal you approach a mooring place, a mini marina. Then the lock itself comes into view and the path goes off to the left into one of the car parks, then the road and your starting point.

The White Swan at Torksey Lock

2. Welton

Route: Welton – Grange Farm – Granary – Dunholme – Welton.
A walk through fields, along some quiet lanes and a streamside path.

Distance: 7 miles.

Start: From the church in Welton. OS Landranger Series Map 121, square 0179.

Getting there: 4 miles north from the centre of Lincoln along the A46, turn left to Welton.

The Black Bull

Despite its good situation, business has never been brisk on the few times I have been here, maybe because it is just a bit disappointing inside. Fortunately the beer is good and they really try hard to make the food different (and good), as well as reasonable in price. They sell all types of steak which vary in size from 5 to 32 ounces! Apparently, this was second home to the `Dambuster' crews from Scampton (where the Red Arrows are) but unfortunately, the memorabilia has been given to museums.

Beers: Ansells and Tetleys. Open 11.30am – 2.30pm Monday to Thursday, 11.30am – 3pm on Friday and Saturday, and 6.30 – 11pm all evenings except for the fairly standard Sunday hours (see Walk 1).Phone: (01673) 860220

Welton

Nowadays this is more a dormitory for Lincoln than any thing else. There is a wide choice of housing and plenty of shops, but not a lot of atmosphere.

The Walk

From the parking area in front of the church, go down the road away from the pub, passing a small green with an old water pump in the middle. Then turn right down a green lane past High Moor House and a bungalow next to it, after which the lane becomes a green lane proper. A little later (and in the spring) the path looks as if it is covered in bark chippings but a closer look shows them to be the `wings' from the seeds of the lime trees by the path. After that there is an `in and out' stile in the corner next to the gate and the path stretches before you on the same line across or along the field sides for a mile and a half.

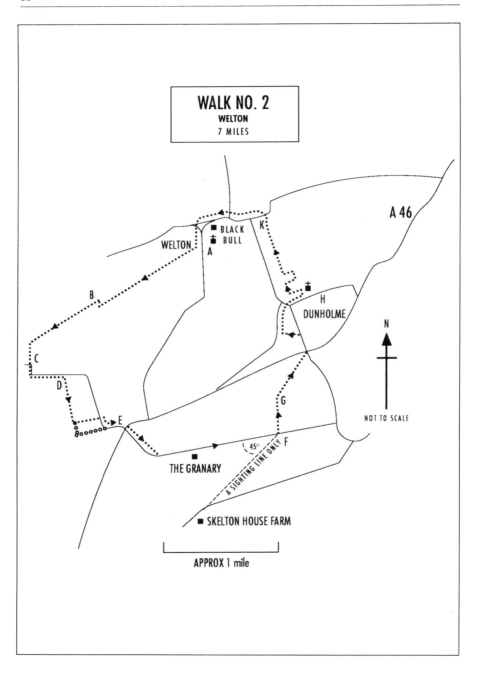

WALK NO. 2
WELTON
7 MILES

A 46

BLACK
BULL

WELTON

A

K

H
DUNHOLME

B

C

D

E

G

F
45°
A SIGHTING LINE ONLY

THE GRANARY

SKELTON HOUSE FARM

N

NOT TO SCALE

APPROX 1 mile

Along the way you pass through a schooling area for would be horse men and women with the equipment for practising show ring, cross country and dressage techniques. As the hedgeside path comes to the water, stiles and the path keep you clear. Watch out when going over the last stile out of here, as electric fencing is apparently occasionally used in the next field and a wire is strung over the branches near the stile.

From there, when the hedge turns to the right away from you, carry straight on. A path had been made over the sown crop but it might not be clear when you go. You will in any case come to a road at (B) and here you turn right and then left, heading for an avenue of trees that stretches away from you. To the right is a very well kept farm and farmhouse while ahead is a pleasant avenue to walk through with a mixture of trees, including early flowering cherry. Once again, some brick `remains' appear, which look rather World War II-ish.

After that, turn right and then left and go along the right-hand boundary of the next field. At the end of it, follow the arrow which points left and through the next gap in the hedge which is the exit to the road in the middle of a series of bends (C). Go left, cross the road and follow it for the next 700 yards or so. This involves passing two small industrial sites before coming to a path at (D), on the right, that takes you straight across the middle of the field. In fact, the OS map says the path goes to the right-hand end of the wood in front so that you can walk to the left as far as the road. It is easier, however, to turn left when you come to a hard surfaced farm road that also takes you to the same road at (E).

Turn right to reach the A46, cross with care and go up the lane opposite. At the top of the rise there is a splendid view as far as the Wolds. From the top of the rise, it is also just under a mile to the path that goes over the fields to your right. If the sign has disappeared, the only indication of where the path might be is by looking to the right and back, where Skelton House farm can be seen. When the sight line is 45 degrees to the road, you should be opposite the start of the path. Once there, at (F), the path is again marked by tractor wheels and continues for two fields until in the third field you might think you are walking over a quarry, as there is so much surface stone.

At the next field boundary, cross the bridge and turn right at (G). It is here that the path aims for the far corner at the top right of the field. Depending on the time of the year and the state of the crop, either take the direct route or carry on to the hedge without turning right and going up to the corner, alongside the road. Once there by either path, the A46 must be crossed once more.

The Four Seasons Hotel on the corner advertises reasonably priced rooms. It has an Italian restaurant, so I presume the head waiter is called Vivaldi! After passing the far end of the hotel car park, take the path on the left which leads to a road. From here the path is right, along the road to the church and over the bridge in front of the church (H). The stream, which comes from Old Man's Head Spring, west of Welton and 200 yards to the north of the first leg of the walk, has a path beside it. Follow it by going to the left and so round the church. At the ford, turn right and after a few yards, turn left, go along the lane, which shortly becomes a green lane until a farm track is joined. Then go down to the left. This track curves round to the right and should be followed to the far corner, where by turning right and curving left you get round the reservoir. By going right after this you will see a path through, between the houses and out onto a crescent. Go left and come out on Ryland Road. All that is required now is a left turn and a purposeful stride without turning off this road, to arrive back at the church, or the Black Bull.

3. Scothern

Route: Scothern – Langworth – Red Barn Farm – Scothern.
A stroll along farm track, road and fields.

Distance: 3½ miles.

Start: Car park in front of the village hall. OS Landranger Series Map 121, square 0377.

Getting there: 3 miles from Lincoln, NE on the A158 turn left onto the road marked Scothern 1½ miles.

The Bottle and Glass

A place that fits the village, comfortable without being flashy. Food is served every lunchtime, usually from 12 until 2, but for half an hour longer on Saturdays and Sundays and every evening except Monday. Beers: John Smiths, Directors and Ruddles. Opening hours: Monday – Friday 12am – 2.30pm, 6 – 11.30pm; Saturday and Sunday 12am – 3pm, 6 – 11.30pm (Sat) and 7 – 10.30pm (Sun). Phone: (01673) 862231

Scothern

Even a Yorkshireman could live here (I think). The people are very friendly and obviously foster a lot of community spirit. There are many very nice houses but not many for sale. When I was there I was told that they apparently have a `shriving bell', a type of call to confession, which was no longer needed for its original purpose after the Reformation, so it was renamed the Pancake Bell and is rung at 11am every Shrove Tuesday.

The Walk

From the car park (A) go towards the pub and turn left to walk up to the crossroads 40 or 50 yards ahead. Turn left again here into Claypool Lane to turn right at the end (B) and walk up to the post office. Slightly ahead on the other side on the road is a grassy path which goes between a hedge and a lapwood fence. Follow this for 30 or so yards to the stile and footpath post at (C). From here take a diagonal path to the stile and post opposite. After the bridge and stile turn right and follow a straight path with the hedge on your right, passing a large dangerous looking dead tree and then the sight of the "nodding donkeys" – pumps wirh counterweights – to your right like a mini-pic of Texas. From here, go over to your left, aiming at the gap between the two plantations (D). The next stile has a double fence; across the road, cross another stile and walk along a track with the edge of the wood on your right.

The 'Nodding Donkeys'

As you come out of this last field to turn left, you will see two large drainage ditches that give you some idea of the drainage task that has always faced this county. By following the lane that runs to the left, you will soon be walking along the front of some large, modern but individual houses. One seems to be the home of a member of the Kawasaki motorbike racing team. However, as a landmark, keep going along the front and then ahead at the next junction. Farm buildings may make you think that a private road is ahead, but West Drive is the one to take and is a public right of way. By keeping to this lane as it bends this way and that, you arrive at the entrance to Sudbrook Park campsite (E), a scout camp complete with assault course; I suggest you turn left and keep walking.

You pass more nodding pumps on your left and then turn right, still along

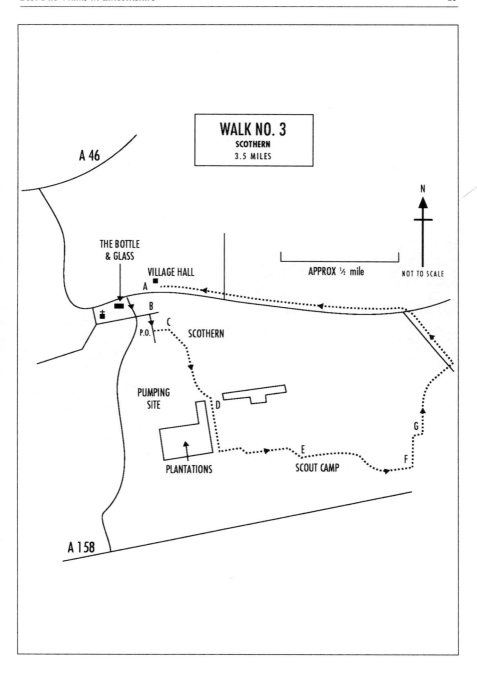

WALK NO. 3
SCOTHERN
3.5 MILES

A 46

N

THE BOTTLE
& GLASS

VILLAGE HALL

A

B

C

P.O.

SCOTHERN

APPROX ½ mile

NOT TO SCALE

PUMPING
SITE

D

PLANTATIONS

E

SCOUT CAMP

G

F

A 158

the edge of Sudbrook Park, and walk to the end of the lane (F). Turn left here and you will see two path signs, one for the footpath and one for the bridleway. Take the bridleway and walk up to the farmyard. When you get there, turn right and go round the right-hand end of the farm buildings (G). There is now an obvious track in front of you so just follow that to the road.

Turn left along the road and left again at the next junction. I like to think that the white bungalow, about here, called `Dawn Run', was bought with the proceeds from a few bets on that gallant little mare. Now, if you wish, you can break into a canter as the car park and the Bottle and Glass are only a couple of furlongs ahead.

The Bottle and Glass

4. Coleby

Route: Coleby – Boothby Graffoe – Navenby – Lincoln Cliffe (Roman Road) – Coleby Easy. Two short sections can be muddy.

Distance: 6 miles.

Start: At road junction next to the Chapel. OS Landranger Series Map 121, square 9760.

Getting there: About 8 miles south of Lincoln on A607, turn right after Harmston. Turn left at the church in Coleby; the chapel is 50 or 60 yards above the Tempest Arms.

The Tempest Arms

Well situated on the edge of the village and the cliff, this pub is open every day and is listed in the Good Beer Guide. Food is served every lunch time and evening in the new 28-seat restaurant, 12am – 2pm and 7 – 9.30pm (9pm on Sunday). Beers: Batemans, Beamish and Courage. Open Monday – Saturday 11.30am – 3pm and 6 – 11pm; Sunday 12am – 3pm and 7 – 10.30pm. Phone: (01522) 810287

The Tempest Arms

Coleby

Once described as `quaint', the village is near enough to Lincoln to have been developed. It is still a pleasant place to live, but is a bit short on amenities (although I did see a bus). It is one of the most attractive villages of those along this cliff, with good views westwards. In addition to some fine looking modern houses and sound looking cottages it has a 17th-century hall built by Sir William Lister, complete with classic styled temple in the grounds.

The Walk

From (A), walk downhill to the narrow opening of the footpath opposite the end of the pub and go left at (B) between a hedge and a stone wall. The path keeps a straight line for three quarters of a mile and is part of the Viking Way. In the second field, the path drops down a little way from the boundary on your left; there are two more stiles to cross here.

The views to the west and south-west are excellent and an added advantage is that the path on the edge of the slope is well drained and for the most part good, easy walking. A stone wall now appears on your left with a stile to climb over as the path goes diagonally over a paddock (C) to the top right-hand corner, past pine trees on your right. Follow the road as it curves through this part of Boothby Graffoe, which has a variety of very nice houses on either side. Ignore the next two turns, one left and then one to the right, walking straight ahead and keeping an eye out for the information board, which is along here on your right. Besides many interesting bits of information it gives a clue to where the stone used for so many of the houses comes from; from the board, you will see that the village has the right to use the stone from the former quarry. The path, in passing Boothby Graffoe, is a mile from Somerton Castle where the Black Prince imprisoned King John of France after capturing him in Poitiers in 1356.

Carry on past the Victorian farm cottages and the farm and go down the lane ahead of you. Here is the village pond (D), some way from the present village, but thought to be sited where the village was pre-Plague. Now it overflows in wet weather and makes the going a bit boggy for a few yards.

The other minor plague just now is the noise of some pretty big military aircraft as they climb out of RAF Waddington. The VC10s certainly have a decibel level of their own, climbing away to your right. You will also see the AWACs planes, occasional contributors to the rising cost of whisky. I'm told that the most popular way of smuggling it into Saudi Arabia was by driving a loaded truck close to the frontier, ensure that it only had a small amount of

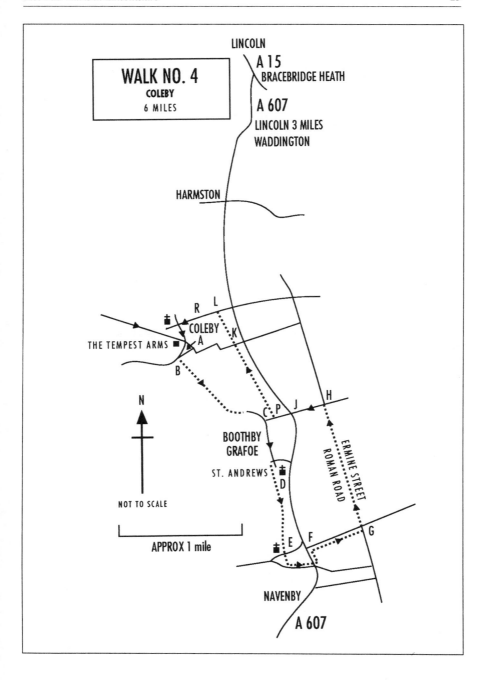

fuel, wedge the accelerator to allow about 10mph, then jump off. A friend would be waiting with a car to drive you through the check point and a few miles further, stop to let you go and look for the truck. Then the AWACs came and had to report all movements picked up near the border. The consequent near drought sent the price of a bottle in 1981/82 from £14 to £50. If you see a walker shaking his fist at a large aircraft with something like a flying saucer on its back, try and guess where he worked.

At the end of that field there is an iron gate that has a stile next to it to climb; cross the next field with the wood on your left, then cross the next one and exit by a path bounded by a post and wire fence on one side and a hedge on the other. After a left and right turn, a stile brings you onto a road. Now turn left, for a walk through the village, walking along the lane called Cat Walk and past the east end of the church (E) before turning left, making your way up to the pub on the left-hand corner and a fish and chip shop on the right-hand corner.

There are plenty of shops here: another of Lincolnshire's surprises is that there is such a wide variety. The date on the old school along the main road is MDCCCXV1.

After a look around (or right away if you are not in the mood for tea rooms, antique shops or art galleries) go left north along the main road until you are nearly out of the village, to take the next turn on the right. Go up this road until you come to a crossroads. The road on the right, High Dike, is metalled, the one on the left (G) is the reason for the slight detour, as this green lane is Ermine Street, the only Roman road in the north of England not to go to London.

When you come to the metalled road again at (H), turn left, go down to the main road, cross over at (J), and then down the road into the village. Shortly after the phone box and just as the road starts to go downhill, go over the small stile on the right and along the narrow path between the houses, then through a little gate, over a stile and across a field towards a large barn. Climb the high stile over a stone wall and go round the right-hand end of the first of the two barns. Now go through a gate and across the fields, heading for the church spire you can see ahead of you. Then, at the end of that field there is a grass track alongside a hawthorn hedge that takes you back into the village of Coleby.

Cross the first road you come to (K) and take the path that runs alongside the wall with its stiles until you have to turn left (L) and go down past a house with stable block and hard tennis court. One more stile and you are out onto the road. Turning right you might hear that you are passing the village junior school before coming out of Blind Lane to turn left towards the church. The roads on either side of the lane are dead ends but do have some nice cottages and houses if you care to look. However, a left turn at the church takes you back to the pub. Slightly to the right is the chapel and your starting point.

5. Bassingham

Route: Bassingham–Aubourn–Bassingham, by way of river bank, green lanes and fields.

Distance: 5 miles.

Start: On the street near the post office and the pub or round the next corner, depending on the day and the traffic. OS Landranger Series Map 121, square 9159.

Getting there: From Lincoln, turn off the A607 at Harmston and follow road through Auburn; from Grantham, turn off at Navenby.

The Five Bells

`Restored' to the present-day idea of a village inn, this pub is clean, pleasant and comfortable but you wouldn't know which county you are in. The menu is above average and the food is good. The beers have been in good condition each time I visited, with a reasonable choice of types and strengths. The wine list is typical of too many English pubs. Still, there are a lot of pubs not run as well as this one. Food is served every lunchtime and evening.

Beers: Theakstones bitter and mild, Morland Speckled Hen, occasional `guest' beers. Open 12am – 3pm, 7 – 11pm weekdays; 12am – 3pm, 7 – 10.30pm Sundays. Phone: (01522) 788269

The Royal Oak

At Aubourn, this is a village pub with documented history. Although reference is made to an `ale wife' conducting her business in the village in 1560, the Royal Oak appears on a map of 1828 as the Plough (the present name appeared in 1870) and surprisingly survived, despite a notoriously drunken landlord, when the other two public houses in the village closed. It is alleged that a ghost has been seen, but it is not recorded which guest beer was `in residence' at the time. The pub plays host to a number of local clubs and societies and serves bar meals every day.

Beers: Batemans (XXX and XB),Tetleys and Sam Smiths plus three guest beers which are changed regularly. Open Monday – Saturday 12am – 2.30pm, 7 – 11pm, with usual Sunday hours. Phone: (01522) 788291

Bassingham

There are times when I think the village life that I enjoy has gone too far. A post office is at least an indication that this one is alive, but it has the feel of a place that you tell everyone at work how wonderful it is to live in, while visitors wonder what on earth do they do there.

The Five Bells

The Walk

Start at the post office (A) and walk northwards up the street (the opposite way to the church) until you come to a T-junction, then turn left again and walk down the road marked to Thurlby. Immediately before a house on the right-hand side (B) you will see a path that appears to go through someone's orchard. It does, so keep to the clearly marked path. The same applies when you come out of the orchard: straight on, over a plank bridge, along the marked way across the middle of this field and along the strip left in the middle of the next field, then over a stile. Now go over to your right as you will see there is another stile almost in the right-hand corner.

The path continues in the same direction along a well worn track with

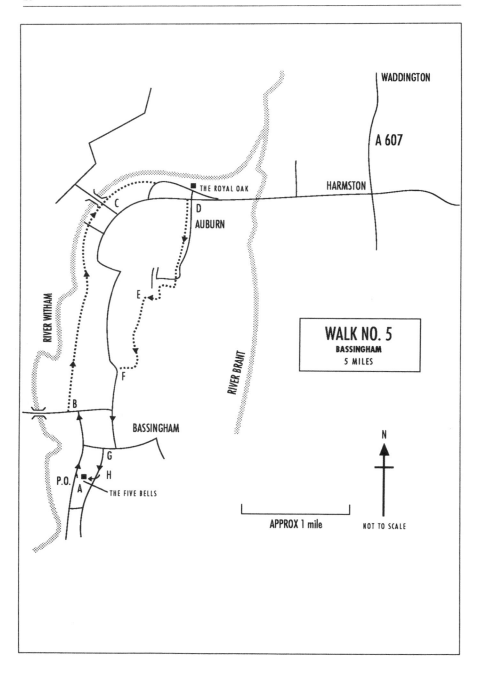

WADDINGTON

A 607

THE ROYAL OAK

HARMSTON

C

D

AUBURN

RIVER WITHAM

E

F

RIVER BRANT

B

BASSINGHAM

G

H

P.O.

A

THE FIVE BELLS

WALK NO. 5
BASSINGHAM
5 MILES

N

APPROX 1 mile   NOT TO SCALE

prominent footpath sign posts in the hedges in front of you. Even without the posts, it is easy to keep the line and after two hedges you find you are pointing towards a gap next to a large tree with a bridge over the ditch there. From that point, the path turns 25 or 30 degrees to the left so that when you reach the high point of the field you can aim at the point where the wood meets the hedge. Fifty yards or so before you get there, turn a little to the right and aim for the third tree in the hedge up from the wood. Go through the gap to the left of that tree and head across the next field towards a lone tree, then across to the far hedge, close to the bottom left corner, through the hedge and on to the bank after passing the weir (C).

Stay on this side of the river following the bank, all the way to the next road bridge, climbing a small barrier along the way, and cross the road there is a stile at either side. Now bear right and follow the hedge line around the field, through the next gap ahead and then as you walk along the next hedge, take the next gap on your right. You will now see there is a stile at the far side if you walk diagonally across this paddock towards the red brick houses. Pass these and walk down the road to the left and to the Royal Oak. If you are there at the right time, you might like to try a taste of the beer. As you will see from the badges on the wall, they are continually changing the guest beers and from those displayed, I don't imagine you will be unlucky. Apart from that, the collection of 300 or so horse brasses just might disturb your concentration on the main business.

Now, visiting or not, leaving the Royal Oak on your left, walk to the junction and turn right, crossing over at the next junction so that you can take the farm road ahead at (D), which is a public right of way. Ignore the turning to the farm and go ahead to the bend that goes right and then left. As you turn this corner, look behind you. The peculiarity of this village is the complete spire with clock, possibly part of a chapter house and little else; it is a good landmark.

Continue, and at the end of the field go into a green lane; where this crosses another lane turn right, and up to an uninviting looking farmyard, where at (E) you turn left into a green lane, over a little bridge at the far end and keep following the track. At the road, go left, bearing left at the next junction, right at the one after that and then left again at (G). There are some allotments on the right and then an open space. Immediately after that, a path goes right between two hedges at (H), and comes out in the car park at the rear of the Five Bells.

6. Normanby-by-Spital

Route: Normanby – Cow Pasture – Saxby Cliff – Owmby-by-Spital – Normanby. Needs a little perseverance and attention to route.

Distance: 4½ miles.

Start: Next to the church and pub. OS Landranger Series Map 121, square 0088.

Getting there: From the junction of the A15 LincolnHumber Bridge and A631 GainsboroughMarket Rasen and Louth at Caenby Corner, go 2½ miles eastwards along the A631 and turn right through Caenby to Normanby by Spital.

The Bottle and Glass

This has the essential ingredient of a pub: atmosphere, which is easier to find in the unspoilt village local perhaps. It is a good reason to use the Bar Room, joining the friendly regulars, that is unless you want a meal in peace. Meals are served lunchtimes and evenings, every day except Monday and Tuesday

The Bottle and Glass

Beers: John Smiths, plus regular changes of the Guest Real Ale. Open Monday – Saturday 12am – 4pm, 7 – 11pm; Sunday 12am – 3pm and 7 – 10.30pm. Phone: (01673) 878378

Normanby

This small village is far enough away from the main roads to have avoided any ruinous development and is just a nice, old fashioned looking village. It does not come as a surprise that the people are pleasant and that you are quickly made to feel at home in the pub.

The Walk

The walk starts by walking towards the church, turning left and walking down to the bridge at (B). It is from here that you have the most difficult part of the walk because the path that goes to the left off the road is difficult. Firstly, the path is blocked by undergrowth; a few yards nearer the bridge you reach the spinney along a path kept open by horses. At the other end of the spinney, the path is not very clear and it needs a brave step when the field has growing crops all over it. But go in a south-westerly direction (or 45 degrees to the left as you come out of the spinney) and when you have a clear view of the plantation that is just over half a mile away, go for a spot about one-third along from the left-hand end, then walk down near to the end (C), cut through the plantation and make for the corner of the field, where you will also be at the corner of the road at (D).

From here on it is plain sailing. Walk along the road to the next corner with the cottage on the left and turn right. It is now half a mile of walking on a wide wide grass verge up to a path that goes across the fields on the left. Power line poles also indicate the place where the path starts at (E). Now go down the edge of the field, keeping the hedge on your right. At the end of this hedge, there is a bit of a kink, left and then right, and you find yourself going down a grass headland between two fields and finishing on a more obvious farm track that takes you to the road. This is Saxby Cliff.

Turn left and walk along the road for nearly a mile. Go through the gap in the hedge at (F), to walk diagonally right over the field to a corner that juts out towards you. From there go to the bank in front of you and walk alongside it to the left. Nearing the wood, look for an easy place to climb the bank to walk to the right along the fields' bottom boundary with the hedge on your right. A short distance ahead, the path joins the one from Saxby which

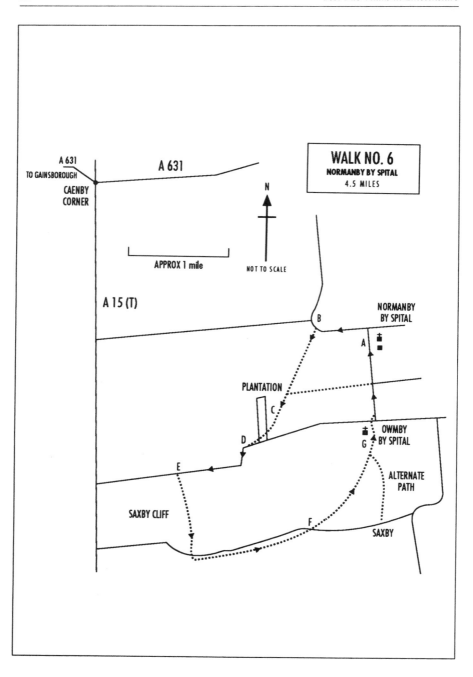

is marked on this map as an alternate path in case of bad weather, high crops or a preference for the easy way. The stile then appears on the left. After crossing, keep the hedge on the right and walk to the other side of the field. The cheering sight of a well kept cricket ground here (G), helps. There is a new scorer's box and a handsome pavilion; the thought of a beer here on a summer's day creates hopes for a good summer. After two more stiles and a slight slope to climb you reach the road. The church is over to the left and the end of the walk is less than half a mile away if you want to stop and look at it. Otherwise, go right on the lane to the road that doubles back to the left so that the road back to Normanby appears to be going to the right. Take the foot-path, ignore the seat and you will be back at the start in 15 minutes.

7. Laughton

Route: Laughton – Blyton – Sandbeck Farm – Laughton Common – Mantree Cross – Laughton

An easy walk along a country road and over fields.

Distance: 5 miles.

Start: At or near the Ingram Arms. OS Landranger Series Map 112, square 8497.

Getting there: From Gainsborough, take the A159 and the third turning on the left after Blyton. From the M180, turn right 5½ miles south, off the A15 from junction 4.

The Ingram Arms

On the main road through the village, the Ingram Arms is a free house selling a small selection of beers in a pleasant interior. It is a popular place for a meal with pleasant staff; the serious drinkers appeared few in number. It is included, not only for the walk, but because the pints I have had there were good and the landlord is obliging to the extent that he says he will always open half an hour or so earlier if a party of walkers ring to say they want a meal. Open Monday – Saturday 12am – 3pm, 7 – 11pm; standard Sunday hours. Phone: (01427) 628465

Laughton

The village does not have anything special to commend it, yet quite a number of people descend upon the place at a weekend. The church shows that someone cared, as the pinnacles on the tower are still in good shape from some earlier attention. They have a cared-for cricket square, so all is not yet lost. It is a place I like to come to, infrequently, providing the stay is not too long.

Blyton

At the other end of the walk, Blyton has an unusual and interesting church. A mother who lost a son in the 1914 - 18 war, killed in Belgium, asked for a Belgian flag and then had it hung above the 13th-century arcades in the church. The vicar then collected the flags of all the Allied nations, to hang there too.

The Ingram Arms

The Walk

Coming out of the car park of the Ingram Arms (A), turn right along a road which is followed for about a quarter of a mile to a left-hand turn. At that point, (B), turn right along the path to near the third telephone pole. From there the path goes left, skirts a small pond (probably, judging by the mounds, once a quarry) which in March is surrounded by daffodils, and then heads towards the church and mill tower on the far horizon. Go down the left-hand side of the field, turning right at the bottom to go on to the bridge. Thirty degrees to the right, cross the field to arrive at (C), a neat little tableau of fence posts, cross bars, and a sturdy looking stile, but no hedge. Now aim for the single tree on your right, then cross the next field and aim for the windmill tower.

A bridge appears, but after that, a little discretion is needed as many of the natural markers on these paths have gone. From the bridge, go right along the hedge until you reach the corner where it angles away, and then come up along the boundary that marks the edge of the sports field to the left until you think you are about half way. From there, turn right and go across to the gap in the hedge at the other side, next to the changing rooms at (D).

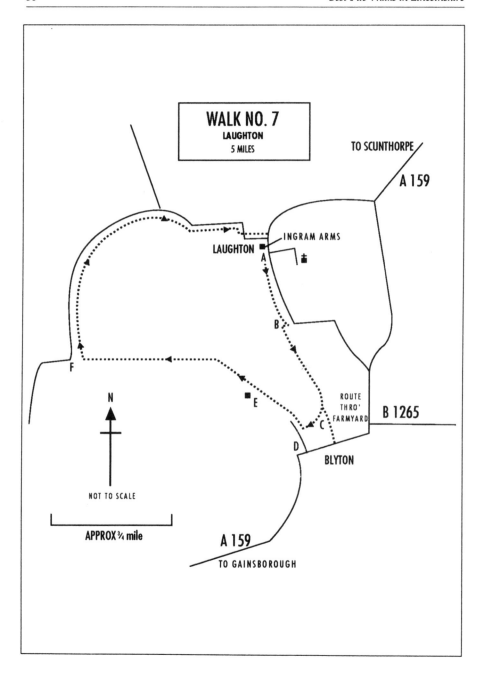

WALK NO. 7
LAUGHTON
5 MILES

TO SCUNTHORPE

A 159

INGRAM ARMS

LAUGHTON

A

B

F

N

E

ROUTE
THRO'
FARMYARD

B 1265

C

D

BLYTON

NOT TO SCALE

APPROX ¾ mile

A 159
TO GAINSBOROUGH

Having gained the road, start walking to the right. A tarmac road at first which, after passing Sandbeck Farm (E), soon becomes a track and then green lane. By following this track you will find you are walking along the left-hand side of a large drain. A wild flower is growing in profusion along the banks of the drainage ditch. Because the soil is sandy over calcareous soils, could this be the pyramidal orchid?

The lane, with the wooded plantations on the right, soon comes to the road proper at a junction that also provides a picnic site. Join the road at (F), and turn right. The woods on either side are a congenial habitat for a great deal of wildlife and for the Brocklesby Hunt.

As the verge is sound and level, enjoy the next mile or so. As you do, approaching the architectural delights of modern Laughton, you may notice signs that indicate the Lincolnshire Cycle Trail – an excellent idea for your next visit to this part of the county. Soon you make a final right turn past the post office to the Ingham Arms once more.

8. Scotton

Route: Scotton – Low Farm – Sweet Hills – Ings Farm – Scotton.

Note: The section from Ings Farm is difficult to navigate without an Ordnance Survey map, and a compass is also recommended. This is because large fields need to be crossed as well as the River Eau and its tributaries; some bridges are missing, probably washed away, which could cause a hasty revision of the route.

Distance: 9 miles.

Start: Near the pub and post office. OS Landranger Series Map 112, square 8999.

Getting there: On the A159 from Gainsborough or Scunthorpe.

The Three Horseshoes

Although this does not serve meals, it is recommended because as soon as you go in the back door from the car park you feel that you are going to enjoy having a drink here. It is a village pub in the best, unspoilt, sort of way and the landlord makes you welcome without fuss. The pub also organises a Fun Run and Gala on Bank Holidays in aid of a local charity.

Beers: Bass Special, Worthington and Websters Yorkshire Bitter. Open Monday – Friday 12am – 2pm, 7 – 11pm; Saturday all day until 11pm; usual Sunday hours. Phone: (01724) 763129.

Scotton

Scotton is so near to the crest of the limestone ridge that Roman legionnaires might have visited the place to break the tedium of their long march along Ermine Street. Their stay was probably short as it is only comparatively recently that afforestation and better farming methods have improved the lot of those attached to the village. At the same time, the quantity and variety of wildlife that flourished undisturbed on Scotton Common when it was part bog and part heather and scrub were much reduced. The Forestry Commission and the Lincoln Trust are trying to reintroduce some species (the Trust having some 40 acres) and save those that have survived so far.

The river Eau flows by the village before going round part of the common on its way to the River Trent. The village church has the old village stocks inside, no doubt to discourage anyone with ideas like Archdeacon Bayley,

`The Goth' as he was known, who plundered many a small village church in the 1820s to decorate his own church at Messingham.

Kirton

You reach the small but bustling town of Kirton in Lindsey halfway around this walk. If you don't feel you have the time during the walk it is worth remembering as a place to drive back to, or visit on another occasion, for there is plenty to see in its pleasant little streets. There are views to the Trent and the Wolds, a 19th-century town hall, built mainly with the material from the old prison, and a whipping post on Spa Hill. William the Conqueror gave the manor and the church to Bishop Romigius towards the endowment of the new cathedral at Lincoln.

The Three Horseshoes

The Walk

From the pub (A) turn left, cross the road and take the next turn right, along a short winding road through a mixture of modern houses. Turn left at the special tree with details of what is so special about it on a plaque below it on the grass verge (B). After half a mile or so, looking to the right, the limestone Lincoln Ridge can be seen; to the left is a windmill, that can frequently be seen working.

A road junction looms up next at (C). Here you have a choice: either take the footpath ahead along the right-hand side of the house, which carries on until it is opposite, but

150 yards from, the small wood on the right and then turns down to the road again. Alternatively, the easy option is to take the quiet road on the right which arrives at the same point after a left-hand bend. Where the path meets the road (at D) take the a path that crosses the field on the right at about 45 degrees out from the hedge on the left, over one field boundary, along the hedge of brambles and on till a farm track appears in front running right to left. Go down it to the left, walking behind some farm buildings to the road.

At the road, turn right and walk under the railway bridge, past the station and after about 400 yards, there is a road through a suburban development at (E). If you keep to this main road through the housing, there is, at the top, a short path over grass, which is followed by a road going right and left. Before you go right (as the walk does) this is the place to stop and consider a short stroll through this bustling little town. The alternative is to come back by car.

The walk, as mentioned, goes to the right and under the railway again. Sail planes or gliders can be seen here, both soaring and being towed up from the airfield on the edge of the town. Soon after the bridge, there is a drive at (F) up to a farm and some other houses. Walking up to these the track turns left (G). In following it, you will notice that this area is very flat, which is why care is needed: adequate drainage can only be achieved with very deep drains. Where a bridge is missing I would not advise attempting to cross in any other way. In one place on the route itself, a telegraph pole had been dropped across the deep dyke, but as I didn't fancy a circus act I added nearly another mile to the walk looking for a bridge. Be sure to carry the OS map, if only to wave at anyone who tells you you are going the wrong way. With a compass you will know that you should follow a line 270 degrees magnetic from the end of the farm track. Notice also how rich and heavy the soil is and how tractors pulling a harrow through the plough have a hard job even with double wheels, front and back.

Go straight ahead at the end of the track to the next hedge. To get to a sound bridge, turn right and walk with the hedge alongside on the right. Over the bridge, turn left and walk along the side of the drain. This is in fact your first contact with the river which goes into the Trent. When two large beams across the river are seen, cross, turn right, and follow along the other side until you come to a group of three or four trees; from there, make for the gap that can be seen in the hedge ahead and opposite. Depending on cropping, either cross the field or circle it by going left, as the spinney to your left front is the next objective.

Go through the spinney and along the farm track to the road ahead, where you turn right and head for the village. Before the church, turn left onto Middle Street, and right at the end of it, to reach the Three Horseshoes.

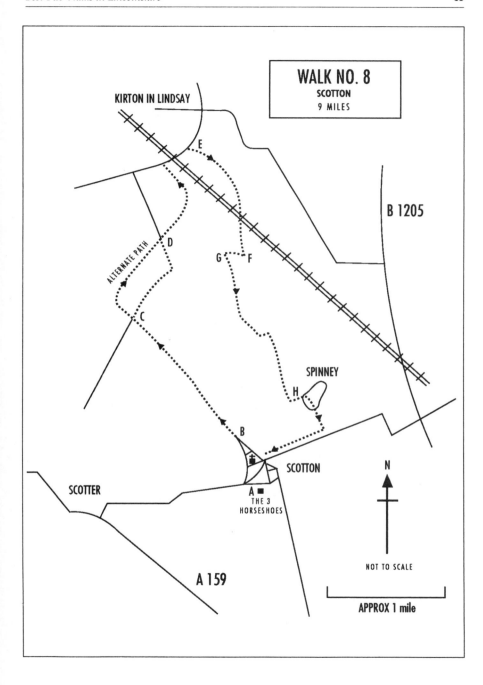

9. Burton upon Stather

Route: Burton upon Stather – The Cliff – Alkborough – Coleby – Burton upon Stather

This walk takes you along a slowly rising path at start, then on mainly level farm tracks and a country lane. Fairly easy.

Distance: 6½ miles.

Start: The Sheffield Arms. There is a car park behind it; the landlord's permission to park is required. OS Landranger Series Map 112, square 8717.

Getting there: From M180 to M181 towards Scunthorpe, across next two roundabouts, and then left at third (with Citroen dealer on your right); follow signs to Burton upon Stather, B1430. Pass Normanby country park on your right and turn left at the next mini roundabout, through Normanby village; one mile further along B1430 is the Sheffield Arms, next to the church. If approaching from the Humber Bridge, turn right at the first road junction after the bridge, follow the A1077 (Scunthorpe) for 7 miles and then turn right onto the B1430 to Burton upon Stather via Thealby.

The Sheffield Arms

A Wards brewery pub, this only sells their beers, which in fairness are very well kept; a point underlined by a plaque on the wall that has been awarded for the cellar work. There are two bars and a dining area where meals are served lunchtimes and evenings every day except Sunday evening. The food is very reasonably priced. In 1999, the menu included steak and kidney pie for £4.60, two dishes for less than that, and a board with interesting specials which, regrettably, no longer include T-bone steaks. Accomodation is available in the pub and there is a Bed and Breakfast just across the road from the pub, phone (01724) 720471. The pub itself is open Monday – Friday 11am – 3.30pm, 7 – 11pm; 12am – 3pm, Sundays 7 – 10.30pm.Phone: (01724) 720269

Burton upon Stather

This village is attractively sited high above the River Trent before it joins the Humber. From here a great deal of Yorkshire can be seen including, on a clear day, York Minster. It has some attractive houses and cottages, the latter a little unusual as they are made of `clunch', a form of chalk. Going down from the well kept church which has very French-looking examples of pollarding in the churchyard, the path takes you to Stather, the name that was given to the ferry. This used to cross the Trent to Garthorpe giving access to Goole. The hamlet used the same name and exists mainly as a place where timber has long been imported.

If you start the walk at about 9.30 in the morning, you should be able to get back in time for lunch and then drive over to Winteringham for the slightly shorter walk there (see Walk 10).

The Walk

Go round the south side of the church after using the gate next to the car park `A', which joins the path from the main street at (B), and go along the tree lined path to the gate leading to a modern residential area. Once through the gate, turn left and go down behind the first house to where a path crosses your front. At this point (C), turn right and join what is now called the Nev Cole Way, as a memorial to a man who joined the Wanderlust Rambling Club in 1932, and devoted much of his life to the preservation and development of the rights of way that you and I are pleased to use. In pre-war Lincolnshire, it must have taken a fairly tough, no-nonsense sort of chap to attempt that.

This path goes along the top of the Cliff, which as you see gives a good view across the river and is well furnished with benches, even though it is too early for you to sit down. Early on you will pass a few houses on your right (one with a chalet in the garden), and then a beacon post before arriving at a bit of a clearing. More benches here. Perhaps a local pastime is mole watching, as over this patch there are some of the biggest molehills I have ever seen. Next, the path takes you along the side of a drain to your right, and after a few more yards, to a bridge (D). Cross this and then turn left. Still following the Cliff, you will see a water tower on your right. Continuing, the path becomes a long but gentle climb and also opens up the view. You can now see, after the flat bit of Lincolnshire, some of the West Riding of Yorkshire, a few more curves of this wide river, the meeting of the Rivers Ouse, Trent and Humber, and the Yorkshire Wolds. You might also see some commercial shipping and realise what the country has missed by not using, maintaining and modernising the river and canal system. Had it been available after Beecham, the constant argument about roads and motorways might have been avoided; as you will see, large barges go a long way down the Trent, and small cargo boats as far as Selby, on the Ouse.

On your right you may have noticed a series of obstacles that are most like the training course of some hopeful cross-country rider. Maybe the fact that

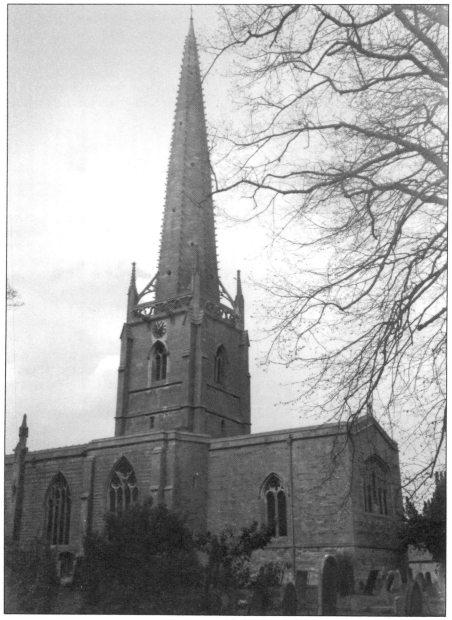

The church at Alkborough

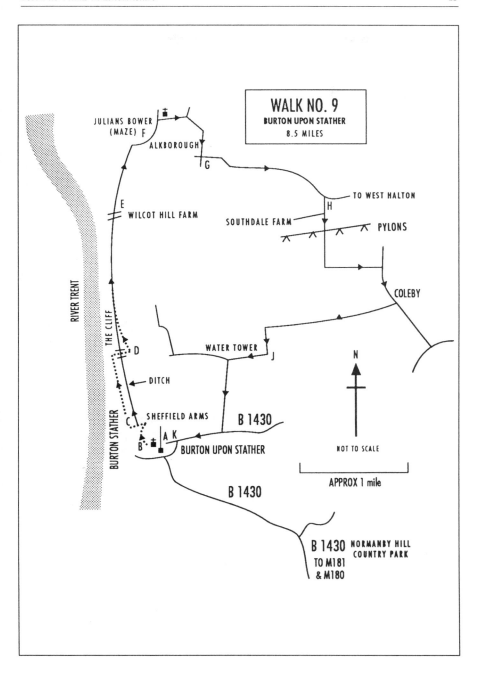

WALK NO. 9
BURTON UPON STATHER
8.5 MILES

JULIANS BOWER (MAZE) F
ALKBOROUGH
G

TO WEST HALTON
H
SOUTHDALE FARM
PYLONS

E
WILCOT HILL FARM

RIVER TRENT

THE CLIFF

COLEBY

WATER TOWER
J

D
DITCH

N

NOT TO SCALE

BURTON STATHER

C
SHEFFIELD ARMS
B
A K
BURTON UPON STATHER

B 1430

APPROX 1 mile

B 1430

B 1430
TO M181
& M180

NORMANBY HILL
COUNTRY PARK

Burghley, with its three-day events, is just over the Lincolnshire border, has something to do with it.

To the left of the path is a notice `Steep bank, beware sudden noise'; whether this is for the benefit of nervous horses or walkers I am not sure. However the steep bank does appear and is easily negotiated, crossing the farm lane (E) up to Walcot Hall Farm, and then up the other side, to carry on along the same path. I managed it without hearing any sudden noise so maybe walkers were out of season.

Soon you will see a path going off to the right, but ignore it. Now the path opens up again and in front of you, in a hollow, is a maze: not the high impenetrable hedge type, but a neatly cut circle with paths about a foot wide to follow in trying to get to the centre. At the far side, a plaque set in a stone cairn saves me any explanation. After the maze, turn right and go through the gap in the wall at (F), and then left and along the road. Unfortunately, the likely looking building on the right is not a pub but the Coronation Social Club, so continue to the church before turning right. This gives you a fine view of the well proportioned church, which is obviously in a good state of repair.

Go along the street past a village shop and telephone box to the junction at (G), and turn left on the West Halton road; keep on the road and pass the old windmill tower over the field to your left. Carry on past the 14 houses on the right-hand side of the road, out of the village of Alkborough and round the right-hand bend. Just as the road turns left (H) take the farm road on the right to South Dale Farm; aim for the pylon do not turn off to go to the farm and about 400 yards after the pylon, the track turns sharp left and takes you down to the minor road. Turn right along this road and go through the village of Coleby more a hamlet than a village, but with few nice houses and cottages especially the unusual house just before you take the footpath that goes off to the right.

Now follow another almost straight track for about a mile. Here the walk feels really good, surrounding you with gently rolling country, trees, a lake in the distance and pleasant views over good farmland. Turn left, still on the track, to the lane at (J). Turn right here up to the water tower, then left along the road towards the village until you reach the T-junction. Turn right up to the next road junction (K). Take the road on the right, marked cul de sac and with a sign for `18th-century conversions'. The road on the left, which curves around to the right, takes you to the pub car park, while the front of the Sheffield Arms is just a few yards along.

10. Winteringham

Route: Winteringham – Haven – Whitton – Winteringham

This is a bracing, sometimes strenuous walk all on the flat – on lane, river bank and open fields. The river bank is high and exposed and the fields after Whitton are over marsh; wellingtons are recommended.

Distance: 6½ miles.

Start: The Bay Horse, Winteringham. OS Landranger Series Map 112, square 9322.

Getting there: From the Humber Bridge, take the A1077 westwards for 5½ miles, turning right at the sign for Winteringham. From M180, go north from junction 4, turn right at the first round-about then left onto B1207 through Broughton, Appleby, and Winterton. After Winterton, one mile ahead cross the A1077. Go straight ahead for another mile to the Bay Horse.

The Bay Horse

After the trip to get here, the Bay Horse is a pleasant surprise. It has a roomy interior with plenty of tables to eat and drink; a function room and dining

The Bay Horse

room have been added without spoiling the look of the place or the comfort of the bar (although it can be a bit crowded at weekends). The large menu, is attractive, changes frequently, and is reasonably priced. En suite B&B available. Patio & barbecue for the summer months.

Beers: four real ales – Wards Best Bitter, Samson and two guest ales. Caffreys, Lambtons, Guinness, Wards Mild and lagers available. Open Monday – Saturday, 12am – 11pm; usual Sunday hours. Phone: (01724) 732865.

Winteringham

Winteringham seems to go shooting out in all directions. I find it is a village of character and some charm, and as it is at the northern end of the Cliff, the land from the village to the Humber is flat. The village is on slightly higher ground and worth looking round. The houses are mostly a mix of Victorian and modern but there are some from the eighteenth century and earlier. The western end of the village is said to be the most attractive. The village possibly has much earlier foundations, as it was here that Ermine Street met the Humber. However, when the end of Ermine Street was sandblocked it became less favoured as a crossing point and South Ferriby surpassed it. In the thirteenth century a bridge was made over the Ancholme at Brigg and traffic diverted to Barton on Humber. Winteringham had some fame later as a staging point between Hull and Gainsborough and at about the same time gained a branch line from the North Lindsey Light Railway.

The Walk

From the pub, turn left down the lane that runs down the side passing the car park; you will see the unusual name of the lane on the wall opposite. It is not much more than half a mile down to the entrance to the Humber Yawl Club compound, the same sailing club that has its main clubhouse at Brough, on the other side of the Humber.

As you reach the gate you will see a bridge on your left, with another gate (A) on your right when you cross. Walk along the entrance lane, turn left at the gate that now confronts you and go past the clubhouse on your left. In a few yards there is another gate (B) which gives you entry onto the flood bank of the River Humber. If the tide is low, you might ask yourself why you cannot walk along the edge of the river as there seems plenty of greenery. Don't try it: these salt flats get covered very quickly when the tide comes in, and with the tangle of rushes and the like, you might not get out.

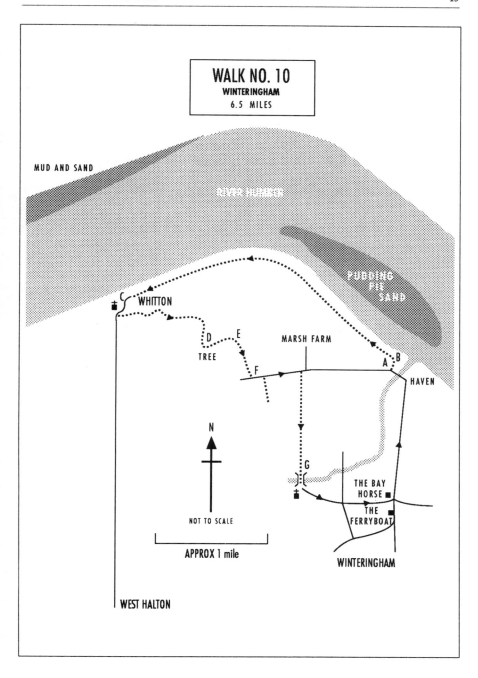

WALK NO. 10
WINTERINGHAM
6.5 MILES

MUD AND SAND

RIVER HUMBER

PUDDING
PIE
SAND

C
WHITTON

D E
TREE
F

MARSH FARM

A B
HAVEN

N

NOT TO SCALE

APPROX 1 mile

G

THE BAY
HORSE
THE
FERRYBOAT

WINTERINGHAM

WEST HALTON

But this high bank does compensate by giving you good views: on your left, the end of the Cliff and then acres of farmland, and to your right, constantly changing river views. At high tide, there is river traffic to inland docks and wharves, and at weekends, yachts from the havens of Brough and Winteringham can be watched cruising or racing. On the far bank, with a backdrop of the Yorkshire Wolds, you can see various industries, most prominently Blackburns, an aircraft company that went public in 1915 and came to Brough after World War I. Taken over after producing their most successful aircraft, the Buccaneer by Hawker Siddeley at the beginning of the 1960s, this is now part of British Aerospace. Just after their factory you can probably see the masts of boats in the haven, the main part of the Humber Yawl Club.

It is about two and a half miles along the path to Whitton with a good path under foot and quite a bit to see. At low tide you can see how fast the tide goes out as it races through the channel between shore and Pudding Pie Island. When the river is high, look for the red navigation buoys which appear to be motoring quickly through the water. Looking back, you can get a wonderful view of the Humber Bridge with its impressive span.

Nearing Whitton, there is a path to your left, but ignore it, as Whitton is worth a look with its winding street, the cottages and houses and unusual church. Arriving there, you climb over a substantial looking stile, go down to the left between hedge and dry stone wall, turn right and walk in front of some pleasant houses. At the point where you join the road, you can take a path over on the right-hand side at (C) which goes up past the church and comes out at the corrugated chapel, back on the lane.

Continue on this lane up to the telephone box and follow the footpath pointer to the left. Curve your way round the paddock on your right and at the end of it, walk over to the post and yellow arrow at the junction with another lane. Turn left and walk up to the bridge and use it to cross the dyke on your right. After this, walk across the field aiming for the right-hand end of the hedge that comes up from the left. From there, go left keeping the field boundary on your left and head for a line of poplars, then past a second group of them to a farm track where you should turn right (D). Ahead of you is a very big tree standing alone at the junction. Turn left and walk along this lane up to the point where there is a large drain going away to your right and some silos on your left (E). Turn right and walk along the left-hand side of the drain up to a small coppice which is now mainly elderberry, and then turn left along the side of a smaller drain.

Cross the next bridge you come to and walk with the drain on your right until you come to the next post and yellow arrow which directs you onto a well surfaced lane running east (F). Although the village is in sight, ignore the first post you see indicating a path to the right and keep on this lane until you are at the place where lane meets road the one up to Marsh Farm and turn right so that the ditch is on your left and the church tower is in front of you. It was along here I came across a small piece of plastic fastened to a little stick, to say that this is a public right of way and that any crops on it would be removed in the spring. This seemed odd, as the council have gone to a lot of trouble to ensure good waymarking, the farmers are not particularly obstructive around here and walkers in such quiet areas are unlikely to `make waves'. I found the answer at the bridge at the bottom of the field below the church; some mindless idiot had thrown the waymarker into the stream and ripped out a section of the bridge's footway! (G).

It is still possible to get over the bridge, after which you should walk up and to the left, then right up Meggitt Lane, to the top by the church gates and turn left. At Weston Green, turn right and keep going until you reach the Bay Horse. This lane has shown you the wide variety of building styles among the houses here and if you have time, a walk around the area can be very pleasant. It certainly shows the village to be much bigger than you first thought.

11. Bonby

Route: Bonby – The Wold – Worlaby – Southwold Farm – Bonby Lodge – Bonby

Easy for nearly all the way

Distance: 8½ miles.

Start: The Haymakers Inn. OS Landranger Series Map 112, square 0015.

Getting there: From the end of the M180, take the first road on the left on the north side of the motorway to Elsham (from the Humber Bridge, it is best to go to the motorway junction and circle the junction roundabout). At the end of the village, turn left and then right onto the B1204 to Worlaby and Bonby. The Haymakers in Bonby is nearly 3 miles from this junction on the right.

The Haymakers Inn

A small pub with two bars (the entrance is at the car park side) that serves a good pint of Tetleys. Food is served from a fairly simple menu at reasonable prices. Attached to the other side of the pub is a fish and chip shop.

Beers: Stones Keg, Tetleys (cask conditioned) plus a changing guest beer. Open Wednesday – Friday 12am – 2pm, 7 – 11pm; Saturday 12am – 4pm, 7 – 11pm; Sunday 12am – 3pm, 7 – 10.30pm. Closed Monday and Tuesday. Phone: (01652) 618793

Bonby

This is mainly a one-street village with a mixture of houses, some of which are tucked away in a lane that run up from the road. The road is busier than most Lincolnshire village roads.

The Walk

With your back to the pub, go to the right past the post office, walking along the footpath on the other side of the road. About 50 or 60 yards after Freemans Lane, a brick rubble-based lane (B) goes up to the left (opposite a long white bungalow). Walk to the top of this lane, go to the right around the back of the houses and then through a gateway into the field. Turn to the left, keep to the hedge on your left and go straight up the field. Over the stile at the top you are confronted with a field that has the path going right over the middle of it. Aim for a point between two large tree trunks that appear to have been gale damaged, using your discretion as to whether you take a straight path or go round the edge, depending on the state of the crop.

Having gained the road, walk along to the left to the double bend at (C), go to the right for about 50 yards and then take the path on the left, by going over the stile. Follow a line to the left of a few thorn trees, then over another stile follow the field boundary to the right as it curves left above some small ponds. In the small thicket ahead you will see, almost hidden, a yellow arrow, confirming that this is where you turn right, through a gap in the hedge and down a short stretch of someone's driveway.

This comes out on a little lane after passing a small orchard and an iron gate at (D), and goes by Worlaby church and Fountain Corner, obviously named as you will see. Walk through this very pleasant part of Worlaby village and take the turn on the left after the telephone box. As this road starts to go uphill you will see the almshouses in front of you. These were built by Lord Belasyce, who fought for the King in the Civil War, raised six regiments at his own expense and then built the almshouses in thanks for his safe return. The village also boasts an avenue of sycamores, but the hall they led to has long since disappeared.

The almshouses

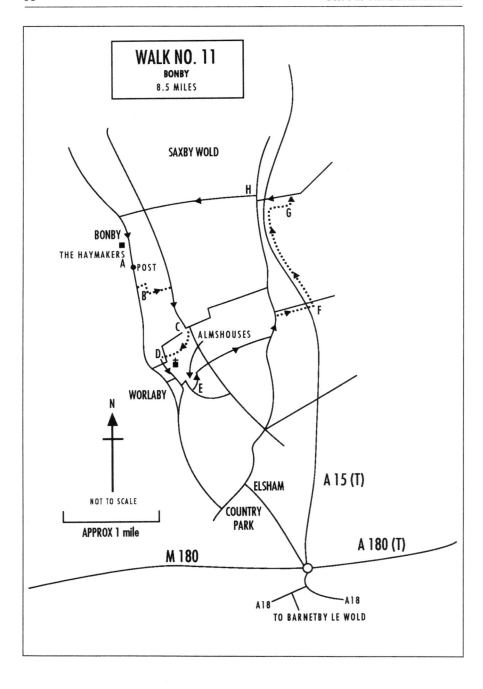

WALK NO. 11
BONBY
8.5 MILES

Now the road bends right and as it gets a little steeper, goes sharply to the left (at E). At the top, it straightens out and a long lane, with some protection from the wind in the form of a stout hedge, takes you over a crossroads and on, until you pass Southwold Farm. After this, take the next left along what is the B1206 and the next right which goes under the trunk road to the Humber Bridge and puts you, for a short way, onto the Viking Way.

Turn left (F) and walk the field edge to Bonby Lodge. At this point, (G), it is necessary to go right, then through a gate that has a footpath sign pointing ahead. Cross this slip road when it is safe to do so and go on to the next junction, so that by turning left you will be able to cross over the trunk road. Having done that, cross the minor road, turn right and then left at (H). This is over a mile long and although the road is narrow, the grass verges are wide and easy to walk on.

After the crossroads, the road continues into Bonby; for safety, as well as easier walking, take the path through the trees on the right-hand side. Pass the church, go round a couple more turns in the road, turn left along the next road and you will see the Haymakers ahead on your right.

12. Barnetby le Wold

Route: Barnetby – the Wolds – Searby – Somerby – Bigby – Barnetby le Wold.

Gentle undulatio. Fairly easy.

Distance: 7½ miles.

Start: Station Hotel. OS Landranger Series Map map 112, square 0509.

Getting there: From the eastern end of the M180, come off southbound on the A18. Within 300 yards, turn right and almost immediately left. After half a mile you will see a railway bridge in front; turn right just before this and go up to the top of the station yard. This is a good place to park.

Station Hotel

Lincolnshire continues to pull surprises. As I nearly always pick the free house, hoping that the landlord has used his choice of beers wisely, that reduces my choice by 50 per cent. Unfortunately, although Stones seems a popular beer in this county, it is not mine and so a few times when walking in this area I have found my choice limited by a brewery. Here in Barnetby, I was left with an old pub in a station yard , that from the outside looked ordinary.

Once inside everything changed. It is a clean, bright, well furnished place, with a good atmosphere, helped by the fact that the landlord and his son made me feel welcome without being effusive or casual. And after all that, the Theakstones bitter tasted very good. Meals are served every lunchtime and on Saturday and Sunday evenings. There is B&B, with 14 rooms available. You could come by train (there are services to and from Grimsby, Lincoln, Doncaster, Sheffield, Hull and Manchester), walk around here, stay the night and then do the Bonby walk the next morning.

Beers: Theakstones, Youngers, lagers and Guinness. Open Monday – Saturday 12am – 4pm, 7 – 11pm, with usual Sunday hours. Phone: (01652) 688238

Barnetby le Wold

These days, few villages have a railway junction and a number of shops beside the post office, but there seems insufficient activity here of any kind to even think of it as a town. It does have two churches, one closed and one a replacement built in the late 1920s. There is also a lead font, one of only 30 remaining in the country.

Just outside the village, on the A18 to the west, are Melton Gallows which were erected on the orders of King James I. Apparently two feuding families of this area were doing too much depopulating for the King's liking, so he decreed that the next member of one of those families to kill one from the others should be strung up forthwith. I notice that they are still kept in a good state of repair!

The Manor House, just off the Viking Way

The Walk

Starting at the station, walk down to the road, turn right, go under the bridge and continue along the main street to the third turning on the right (A). This curves away to the left and just as it has gone through 90 degrees, a footpath sign is obvious, pointing to the left. Follow its direction along a farm track (after the houses) and then turn left after the farm buildings. You will shortly reach a road. Crossing it, take the signposted path to the left of the garage and walk in front of some houses to a stile at (B). Over the stile, go straight ahead and upwards; as soon as you can see the far hedgerow, veer a little to the left to the corner bounded by a post and wire fence and the hedge. Cross the stile, keep the same line with the hedge on your right until you reach the road at (C), from where you can see an old windmill building; then turn right, along the road, ignoring the road that goes down on your right (and the footpath opposite) until you reach a road junction, where you carry on straight ahead.

You will have seen that you are obviously on chalk land typical of the Wolds; now you are on a green lane, typical of the well drained area. It is also a registered caravan site, so obviously more popular than one would think when walking here in early April. This takes you, with a little bit of up and down walking, for about a mile, when after ignoring all other turnings you arrive at the junction at (D). Here there are some pleasant diversions in the form of ploughed and grazing; as the lane passes the approach lights for Humberside airport there is also the faint possibility that low flying aircraft will disturb the peace.

Walk right on to the T-junction at (E) and turn right. There are lovely views ahead of you, as you pass farm buildings and a house and come eventually to the main road (F); you should cross, walk to the left and go down the road on the right. This is the hamlet of Searby and if you take the next turn on the right, you will pass the Manor House. Just after a left-hand bend, there is a gate on the right for you to go through to follow a path across the field. It is here that you can really see the wonderfully understated beauty of the house, with an outstanding balanced facade.

The path you are on now is part of the Viking Way. After the first stile in the right-hand corner, the path is straight, crossing one more stile before coming to a very muddy gateway and the short stretch to the stile that lets you out onto the lane. From this point just follow the lane until you pass a tiny church on your left (which has thousands of snowdrops in the churchyard in the early spring) and then watch out for the stile on the right-hand side of the road at the next bend. Go over this stile and pass the monument so obviously placed (at G) and built to celebrate 29 years of marriage of the lord of the manor. Why 29 years, I know not, but I do like the bit on the plaque that will explain all.

Now, continue to Bigby by walking a curving line which is parallel with the road below. This will bring you to a double stile and stepping stones and, across the next field, a road to cross. Now walk up the road opposite and take a look at the village. Although it has nothing much in the way of amenities, there are some nice houses, many with strikingly big gardens.

By staying on the road out of the village for about half a mile, a sharp

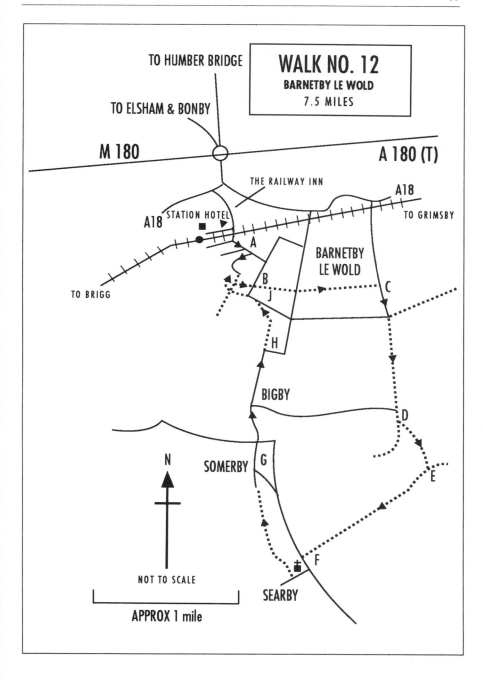

TO HUMBER BRIDGE

TO ELSHAM & BONBY

WALK NO. 12
BARNETBY LE WOLD
7.5 MILES

M 180

A 180 (T)

THE RAILWAY INN

A18

A18   STATION HOTEL

TO GRIMSBY

TO BRIGG

A

B

BARNETBY
LE WOLD

C

j

H

D

BIGBY

N

SOMERBY

G

D

E

NOT TO SCALE

F

APPROX 1 mile

SEARBY

right-hand bend is reached. In the corner facing on the left is a footpath sign (H), for you to follow in the direction of the church you can see on the sky-line. When you reach the corner of the field, your path is downhill to the left. Part way down is an arrow marking the point to turn right and cross diago-nally to some old sheds and then onto the road (J). On the road, go left, then turn right at the bottom; a little further along turn left, bringing the garage on the other side of the road into view. This is the garage passed on the outward leg, so turn left down the lane, along the field track, right at the farm build-ings and back to the station.

13. Bardney

Route: Bardney – Southrey – Bardney

A walk along roads, farm tracks and through woodland.

Distance: 6 miles.

Start: Village cross at road junction. OS Landranger Series Map 121, square 1169.

Getting there: From the A158 at Wragby, take the B1202. From Lincoln, take the A15 and then the B1190.

There are three pubs in the village. I like this one the best:

The Black Horse

The fourteenth-century Black Horse is a committed pub. When I was there, it served no food, but sells a great pint of three of Theakstones best, Batemans and a guest beer/real ale. Open Monday – Saturday 11am – 3.30pm, 6.30 – 11pm; Sunday 12am – 3pm, 7 – 10.30pm.Phone: (01526) 398900

Bardney

The village appears busy, mainly because of the road coming over one of the few bridges on the Witham. But it has industry in various forms and the village centre seems to be a lively hub set at the junction, with market cross, shops, church and pubs close at hand. On a green of sorts is a modern, but nevertheless impressive, memorial in the form of a three-bladed propeller, typical of those fitted to the bombers that flew on so many dangerous missions from the local base.

The Walk

The start is near to the newsagent's. If you face the church, go along the road to the left (from A) heading for the large wood you can see ahead and to the right. A farm lane opposite some cottages at (B) marks the lane to walk until you get to the corner of the wood. At that point, turn left again and follow the edge of Southrey Wood. The path curves around a little way to the right; at

The memorial on the green at Bardney

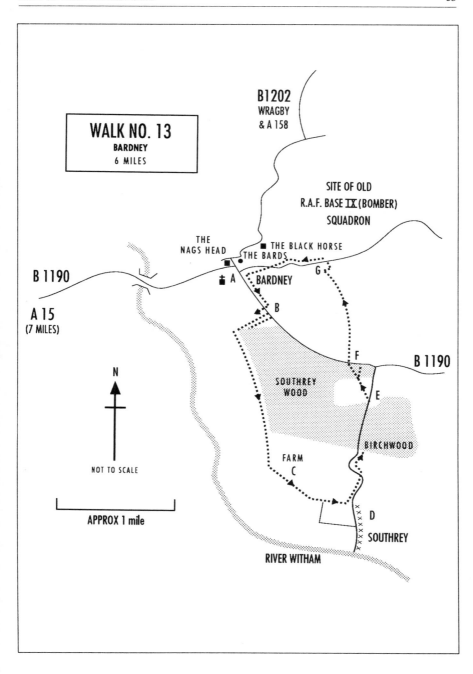

WALK NO. 13

BARDNEY

6 MILES

the end of the field on your left, turn left and go down a farm track, round and left again passing Poplars Farm (C). When you see a beautiful farmhouse like this, you really know that the farmer has earned it. The place smacks of efficiency and after all, they are improving the environment as well as preserving a fine building.

Keep going along the road to Southrey village to the junction with Ferry Road, where the walk goes to the left (D). If you can spare 10 or 15 minutes, turn right first and walk down the 500 yards or so to the river just to see some of the cottages in the village.

Back on the proper route, the road snakes a bit before running between the two woods. When you come out at the other side, look to your left for the path which has a wicket gate (E). Go through it, up the edge of the field, through the second part of the wood by a house that has three very noisy dogs.

Once out of the wood, cross the road at (F), and go over the field opposite to the back of those farm buildings you can see ahead. At (G) take a right and a left around the farm and out onto the road where a left turn and a walk of a little more than half a mile will bring you back to the start.

14. Rothwell

Route: Rothwell – The Park – Mount Pleasant – Nettleton Beck – Rothwell

Excellent walking through varying landscapes.

Distance: 7½ miles.

Start: Centre of village, at road junction, facing the road to Binbrook. OS Landranger Series Map 113, square 1599.

Getting there: From Grimsby, take the A46 to Swallow, then turn left and follow signs to Cuxwold and Rothwell. From Market Rasen, take the B1203 heading east-north-east and turn left in Binbrook, to follow signs for Thoresway and Rothwell.

The Nickerson Arms

This pub is a reflection of the village in many ways. Well kept and friendly, it bears the name of the village's most successful family in modern times. It has an extensive range of beers which do change but not frequently: it has Theakstones, Boddingtons, Tetleys, and less well known names too, well worth trying as the landlord is obviously a good judge of beer. Current fashions are also catered for with Belgian brews and a range of lager and strong bottled beers. It is especially heartening to see a good range of wines for sale at reasonable prices. With imaginative menus for lunchtime and evening meals, it is a shame that there does not appear to be any accommodation available in the village, so one of you is going to be on soft drinks! Incidentally, the pub plays host to the Grimsby Harriers Annual Charity Race early in July each year.

Open Monday – Saturday 12am – 2pm, 5 (6 on Sat) – 11pm; Sunday 12am – 3pm, 7 – 10.30pm. Phone: (01472) 371300

Rothwell

Situated in a dip in the Wolds, this is a neat and prosperous looking place, complete with stream and a Victorian mansion, Rothwell House. The park, just past the church, was opened to the public years ago; apparently the fountains at the Nickerson house play every Sunday, money having been left for their upkeep because local people like to sit around them. The man responsible, Joseph Nickerson, was described to me as hard but fair: when asked in later years by an old school friend how he had become such a successful businessman, "because I don't remember you as being all that bright when we were at school together", he replied, "You might be right, but I know how to delegate and I'm lucky enough to pick the right people." A key to success maybe, but it sounds very modest for a multi-millionaire.

The Walk

From the road junction (A) described above, walk along the Binbrook road past the church. Shortly after the left-hand bend in the road there is an entrance to parkland (B) on the right. It is well signposted and passes ponds with ducks, fairly tame pheasants, spinneys, and grazing land. It is very pleasant walking and easy most of the way with just one or two climbs. But keep to the path and don't be tempted by the stiles you pass on the right.

Rural scene above Rothwell

In countryside as good as this you may feel tempted to do an extra mile or so. If this is the case, there is a bridleway at (C) going off to the left where the farm road turns to the right. It goes up what is Thoresby North Wold , meets the farm road to Hills Brough Farm and by turning right twice, brings you back to meet the path that you are on now (marked as an alternative on the map) at Mount Pleasant.

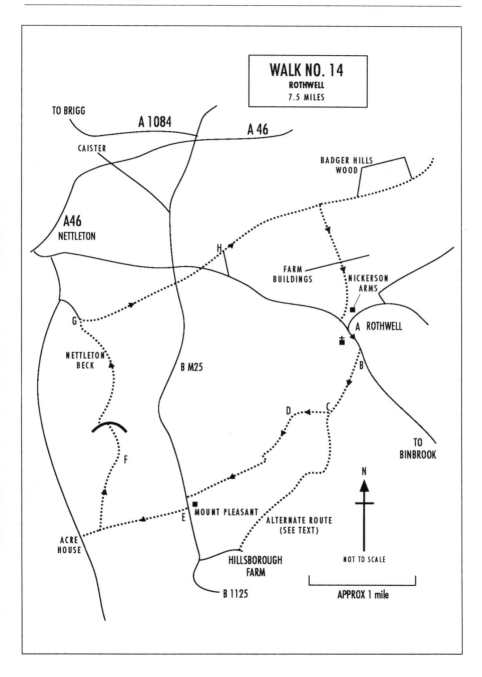

TO BRIGG

A 1084

A 46

CAISTER

BADGER HILLS
WOOD

A46
NETTLETON

WALK NO. 14
ROTHWELL
7.5 MILES

H

FARM
BUILDINGS

NICKERSON
ARMS

G

A ROTHWELL

NETTLETON
BECK

B M25

B

D

C

TO
BINBROOK

F

N

E MOUNT PLEASANT

ALTERNATE ROUTE
(SEE TEXT)

ACRE
HOUSE

NOT TO SCALE

HILLSBOROUGH
FARM

B 1125

APPROX 1 mile

After going right with the road, a short straight stretch takes you to a gap, marked (D), between two areas of woodland. Immediately after that, turn left and walk up the hill to pass the buildings of Rothwell Top Farm and then to the road.

At the road, turn left until you come to Mount Pleasant, 200 - 250 yards away, and there turn right (E) onto the path that follows field boundaries along a broad grass strip until you almost get to Acre House. In fact what, you will see is the hedge on your left, curving in almost a semi-circle on your left, while on your right, after a bit of a hump, is the wide end of a funnel, which is the opening into the dale. Turn right here and walk downhill. You will also notice the high tension wires that run overhead and draw your attention to the correct route, which is a part of the Viking Way.

As the valley begins to flatten out, there is a hedge corner on your right and to the right of that corner a stile (F). Cross the stile, and as you walk a little to the left, the path goes along beside Nettleton Beck. When a small area of woodland is reached, cut through it, going to the right a little to the mouth of a tunnel. This, and the one on your right that is blocked up, were once used for a small railway that brought wagons from the quarry to the road ahead. So go through the tunnel, up a slight incline to the right and forward to the road side and the stile.

Having crossed the stile and road, go left for a few yards and then right into more pasture land, to continue downhill with a post and wire fence on the left. A beck confronts you and the stile and bridge combined lead into the next part of the dale which goes to the left. The path that you should now seek starts to the right, opposite the farmhouse at (G) (the next building on the left). From here it is a mile or so of steady uphill walking, with the benefit of tremendous views each time you look around as you get higher. The path goes on in a straight line, but near the top does cross two roads. The gaps are obvious so there should not be a problem. Go just a little way into the field before going across the middle of a field, then to the left a little to join a farm track at (H). Stay with this track until you reach a crossroads" of paths and turn right.

You are now on the path that will take you down into Rothwell, crossing a farm road when you are on the left of some farm buildings and their protecting trees, to arrive just a little way above the Nickerson Arms. This is definitely one of the best walks.

15. Binbrook

Route: Binbrook – Stainton le Vale – Kirmond le Mire – Thorpe le Vale – Binbrook.

Note: Carry an OS map, for route marking in this area and the next village, Tealby, is almost non-existent.

Distance: 8 miles.

Start: In the open area, (where parking is possible) opposite the manor house. OS Landranger Series Map 113, square 2193.

Getting there: 7 miles north-east of Market Rasen on B1203.

The Plough

On the opposite side of the road to the manor house and further down to the right, this is a small, fairly typical village pub, with rooms of odd shape branching off from the bar. It is modestly furnished except for the room at the front which you are encouraged to use when eating. It is not clear why the other pub closed as it was on the main road through the village and owned at the time by the same brewery.

Beers: Bass, Worthington, Courage Directors and John Smiths, plus Guinness and lagers.

Open Monday – Saturday 11am – 3pm, 7 – 11pm; Sunday 12am – 3pm, 7 – 10.30pm. Phone: (01472) 398241

Binbrook

Once a market town this now ticks over without too much effort. It is in a good setting in a valley with a green on the hillside and surrounded by excellent Wolds scenery. As well as once having two pubs, it used to have two churches. Now there is only the nineteenth-century one carrying the names of both Saints Mary and Gabriel – a good Christmas double act.

Just outside the village, at what used to be RAF Binbrook, an effort is being made to attract more people to the area. A small industrial site, a training centre and quite a bit of money is going to the site, which seems a good idea as there are three towns (Grimsby, Louth and Market Rasen) all more or less equidistant. Being surrounded by beautiful countryside is not enough to make a place the ideal village to live in; to me, the village seems big enough and old enough to take a fresh look at itself. Why not restore the old market for a start and then see if more can be done if it improves business generally? It is a place that deserves to do better without it being necessary to ruin the village way of life.

The Plough at Binbrook

The Walk

From the start, walk up to the main road (left if you are facing the house), turn left past what was the Marquis of Granby up to the junction of the Market Rasen and Orford roads (A) and turn left again. On the right-hand side of the road there is a detached house in red brick, with a footpath sign at the foot of its drive. If the sign is `lost' you will be able to see the stile (B) at the far end between sheds and greenhouse. Go over the stile and cross the grass field to a metal gate with a stile beside it. In the next field, aim for the left of the second post of the power line coming from the left. As you go over the brow, you will be able to aim for the gap in the corner. Through the gap and taking a diagonal line to the right you will come to the corner of the field where there is another gap. Take a few paces to the right and then turn right towards a three-barred stile can be seen. After crossing the stile, walk down-

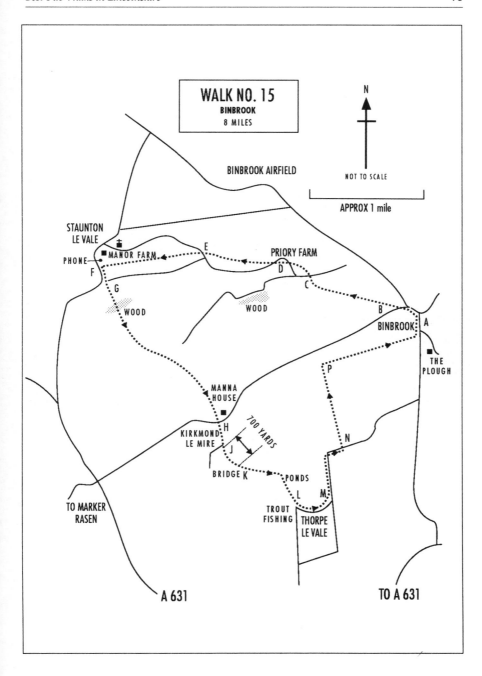

hill and slightly right to (C), the sedgey looking area near the stream. Fortunately there is a walkway followed by a bridge over the stream. Go up the bank until you see the stile on your left; climb over this, and walk a little nearer the farm buildings. The course of a second stream can now be seen going down to the left to join the one you have just crossed. For this one, cross near the bend at (D), so that to keep the line to walk, you go over the water-course twice.

You are now facing west but should follow a slightly curved track, keeping the stream course on your left, to a point where two channels converge. Cross the one that comes from the right, at (E), and walk a straight line for the bottom left-hand end of Manor Farm, before coming out on the road near the phone box (F). Turn right and go down the road as far as the sharp right turn in the road, and at that point take the path on the left to head for the middle of the wood ahead. After the wood, the path curves left for a short way before making a wider arc to the right. This then follows the low ground near the stream and goes through the group of buildings ahead (H) which make up Manna House. Cross the road and follow the track. At (J), where it passes the end of another track on the right, the bridge to be crossed is 700 yards ahead on the left from this point. Take care, as it is easy to miss, which would add two or three miles to the walk (K).

Once across, the route is fairly straightforward along a worn path between the ponds. This brings you to (L), which is the trout fishing place at Thorpe le Vale. Turn left here, to the left of the farm buildings, until you come to the farm road going uphill till it reaches the road at a `Trout Fishing' sign (M).

Turn left, walk up to the next bend, turn right and then go along until you can turn left up a tractor track along the field side with the hedge on the right (N). On the way you will see a footpath sign pointing to the right with farm buildings some way down. Ignore it and keep going in the same direction until you can see that the main road is ahead. Take the signposted path to the right (P).

When you are facing the right direction the church will be visible ahead. There is a nice easy path all the way down until in the last, grass, field, the path turns to the left to go around some dilapidated old outbuildings, takes you down a grass path and to an equally broken down old gate. Go onto the road, walk to the left, and on reaching the starting place, the Plough is down to your right.

16. Tealby/Market Rasen

Route: Tealby – Risby – Market Rasen – Race Course – Tealby Thorpe – Tealby.

There is one fairly modest gradient to walk up. Take your OS map, as except for an occasional Viking Way marker, there is very little help from waymarkers on this path.

Distance: 8½ miles.

Start: As you may wish to park in the village, start on the pavement of the main road, opposite the church. OS Landranger Series Map 113, square 1590.

Getting there: Market Rasen is easy to get to by main roads from all directions, and by train from Lincoln and Grimsby. For Tealby, from the traffic lights at the crossroads near the railway bridge, take the B1203; and Tealby is on the left after 3½ miles.

The Kings Head, Tealby

An attractive thatch-roofed building at the lower end of the village, this claims to be the oldest pub in Lincolnshire. The rooms are not large so that the tables are soon occupied, which makes having a meal at the weekend a bit chancy unless it is fine enough to go out into the garden. The regular beers seem to be Ruddles, Directors, and John Smiths, all a few pence more than average, a fact balanced out somewhat by the fact that the food is certainly above average. It is still a pleasant place to drink, but if you like standing at the bar, you will need to go mid-week. Phone (01673) 838347.

The Old Barn

This is clean and comfortable but ordinary. The meals looked good and reasonably priced and the drinks are a shade cheaper. However, the choice was between Batemans and three different strengths of Everards. There is plenty of room, but the Kings Head seems to get more trade.

Both pubs are open 11am – 3pm and 7 – 11pm, with the usual Sunday times. Phone (01673) 838304.

Tealby

Everyone seems ready to tell you that this is the most beautiful village in the Lincolnshire Wolds with its stream sorry, river running through it and houses of mellowed limestone and brick. It is certainly pleasant enough, and two or three pleasant walks around the area can be started here. Its associations with Tennyson stretch the imagination a bit as the Poet Laureate's grandfather lived at Bayons Manor but left the property to Alf's father's brother; the house was demolished 30 years ago.

The author at The Kings Head

Market Rasen

Although not beautiful, this town has an atmosphere I like. Although it looks like a market town, you don't expect anyone to go rushing around. In the centre there are four pubs almost within crisp-throwing distance of one another, and there are others not far away. The town was one of the two main areas that got the Lincolnshire Rising going, which was reportedly a rebellion against Henry VIII's policies. It was over in two weeks, but during that time it earned the royal rebuke that "people of that one shire ... the most brutal and beastly of our realm". This description was as far from the truth then, as it is now.

This small market town gets its name from the River Rase and holds race meetings at the course less than a mile from the town centre. While participating may be the good fortune of a few, spectating at a jumping meeting as well run as this one is an alternative to walking, worth occasional consideration.

The town is sheltered by woods and Wolds, has a golf course, a few pubs worthy of note and, quite unusual, a school that still receives funds from an endowment set up in the fourteenth century by Thomas de Aston, then canon of Lincoln.

The Walk

From (B) (A is anywhere in the village) go to the left, cross the road and follow the curve of the road for a few yards until you come to a white house on the right and just after it, its garage, built longways onto the road. The entrance way (C) at the end of it is the path to be taken, making your way to the rather heavy and awkward gate at the top. Now walk across the field. The path is fairly easy to see as is your first objective, the wood above Castle Farm. The view to the left is fantastic: even on a day when the weather is poor, it must be worth the walk along here.

The next stile is down in the left-hand corner; once over it, continue over the next field with the hedge on your left. Go past a large pile of rocks, through the gate on the left and up the dale. Make your way up to the right and follow the path through the wood (D) above the farm. The path comes out of the first part so that you walk along the top border, and by keeping a straight line goes into the last part of the wood to the other side where, once over the stile there at (E), the path goes on for a little way along the bottom edge. From there, the path drops a little way to below the buildings which are all that is left of the hamlet of Risby.

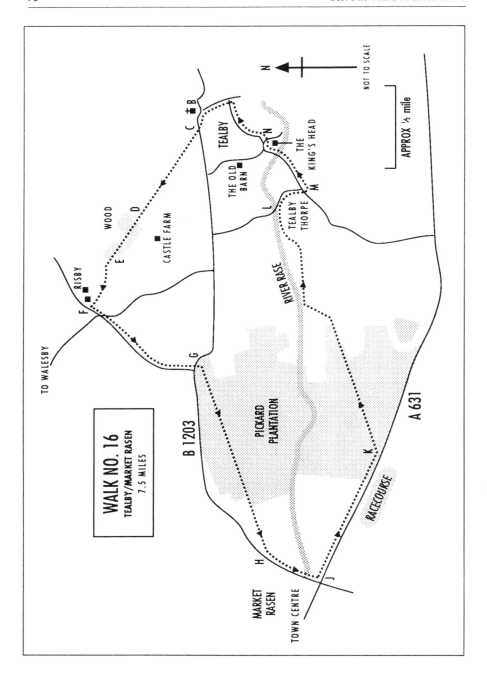

Turn left onto the farm lane at (F) and go downhill, over the road and along the track opposite, and past a house before reaching the road. Turn left, then cross the road and at the corner where the road turns right, (G), there is a path pointer pointing back along a path through the forest.

Stick to this path for about a mile and a half, when you should come to the road as it bends slightly, going left towards the traffic lights. This is the point where you could, if the time is right, stop for a sandwich or a drink.

The return route now means a walk of about a mile along the side of the road, which calls for a left turn at the traffic lights. The forest starts again at a point opposite the middle of the racecourse, and the path starts on your left-hand side, 600 yards after that at (K). Once in the woodland, the path goes straight until it reaches the boundary. When it comes out, it swings 45 degrees to the left and then continues to the right parallel to the bank of the river. It moves away to cross a bridge and then comes back in again to meet the road near the ford. Here turn right, left at the next junction and walk along the road for a quarter mile, back into the village.

17. Donnington on Bain

Route: Donnington on Bain – Gayton le Wold – Biscathorpe Village – Viking Way – Donnington

An occasional gradient, but nothing arduous.

Distance: 6 miles.

Start: By the church. OS Landranger Series Map 122, square 2382.

Getting there: From Market Rasen, go right on the B1225 from the A631 for 4½ miles before turning left for Donnington on Bain. From Louth, take the A153 to Horncastle, turn right after 1 mile and drive through the Wolds via Hallington.

The Black Horse, Donnington on Bain

The Black Horse has a clean, functional appearance from the outside, but the inside reveals that this eighteenth-century inn wears a new coat and the inside is still a village inn. Perhaps slightly overdone inside, it remains popular with the customers. A mural depicts Vikings on the Viking Way, which runs through the village; so walkers can also be assured of a welcome. The food is reasonable and the beer well kept and served, selling what seem to be the three obligatory beers for this area, Directors, Ruddles and John Smiths, plus Adnams. Accommodation is also available.

Open Monday – Saturday 11.30am – 3pm (2.30 during winter months), 7 – 11pm; usual Sunday hours. Phone: (01507) 343640

Donnington on Bain

A nice little place, Donnington is set on one of the few rivers that start and run through the Wolds. Encircled by these Wolds, it seems both independent and secure and with its surviving 700-year-old church, thriving school, two shops and a decent pub. Its valley gets snowed up occasionally.

A strange custom that the village had was the throwing of hassocks, by old ladies, at the bride as she walked up the aisle. It was, I imagine, fortunate that one hit the vicar, who then stopped the silly practice. But that was in the late 1700s.

The Walk

Facing the post office, turn right at (A), and walk up this lane towards a beech hedge. Go left along the path, around the back of an outbuilding, right and then left. At the bottom of the garden go straight on for a bit, between hedges. As you reach an opening by the trees, go into the field and turn left along its boundary. At the far end, turn right and go along with the hedge on your left.

The Black Horse

Now there is a gentle climb up onto the Wolds. A little more than halfway up this side comes a wooden bridge across the ditch, taking the path to the left. Go straight up the field side until a stile is reached on the right,, cross it and the farm track (B), then the stile at the other side, and turn left. Now walk along that path to the road.

When the road is reached, go to the right, still going uphill, pass the entrance to Glebe Farm and look ahead to see the footpath sign ahead on your left (C) where the path turns and goes towards Grange Farm. There is a good surface under foot. Following the path which skirts to the right of a smaller field in front, go through the gap you can see in the hedge.

Carrying on along the border of the next field, there is a great view to your

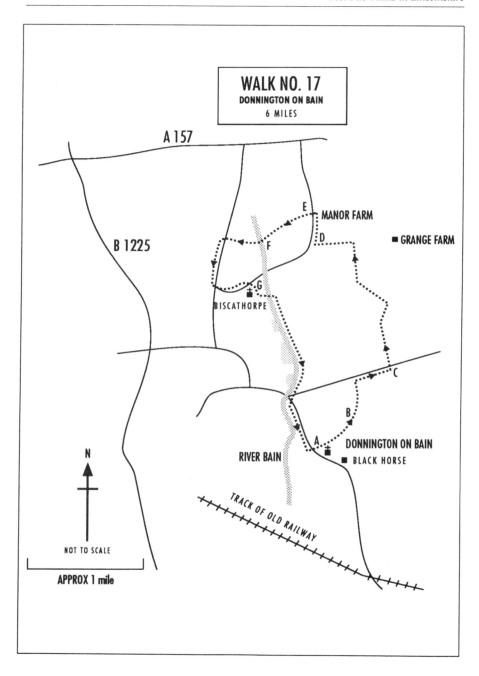

left. Then there is a tractor track to follow and a hedge that starts on your left. At that corner with its yellow indicator, turn left down the road and turn right at (D), having noticed the stone quarries on the other side of the valley. About half a mile along the road you will first pass a house on your left and then Manor Farm on the right. Opposite the farm there is a gate and stile (E). Once over this and in the field, go straight ahead and then angle off to the left to an obvious gate along the left-hand boundary.

When you have got through the gate and reshackled it, head for the far right-hand corner, where there is a bridge and stile to cross (F). The path now takes a diagonal track across the next field to the far corner, when you can see the quarry. Once out onto the track, go to the right and turn left at the road. This is the road to Biscathorpe.

After half a mile of peaceful walking, a side road curves away to the left and will lead you to the church. Go past the house, turn right to go round the far side of the church, then around the back of that church (G), so that you come to a gate in the corner. Through this and head down left towards the river, where there is a bridge to cross. This swiftly running stream is in fact the River Bain and by turning right the path can be followed to Donnington on Bain. On the way, the river widens out into fishing ponds and eventually reaches a very wide pond, a dam with spillway and what appears to be a jetty. Keep to the left-hand side of the river, go through a few trees and along a raised bank and pathway; after one short straight stretch and, opposite a large old tree, the water mill house (reputedly haunted), you reach the gate and the road.

Turn right to the junction and left back into the village, passing on the left what looks to be the home of a competitor in the touring car class. Around the corner there is first the shop, then the church and then the Black Horse.

18. Little Cawthorpe

Route: Little Cawthorpe – Hougham Wood – Burwell – Muckton – Legbourne Wood – Little Cawthorpe

Well signposted and only slight inclines.

Distance: 7 miles.

Start: The church, Little Cawthorpe. OS Landranger Series Map 122, square 3583.

Getting there: Take the A157 from Louth and after passing the B1200 to Manby, take the right-hand road where the A157 turns sharply left.

The Royal Oak (The Splash)

This is a nice looking free house surrounded by a well kept garden, spotless inside without being clinical, serving a good pint with friendliness. The landlord responsible for the buzz is from Oz! I think Australians and Yorkshiremen are a bit alike just on our good points, so I am not surprised that I liked the place. Plenty of others there seemed to feel the same, partly due no doubt to the landlady's touch with the food, which, a customer told me, was very good. Beers: usually Directors, Ruddles, and Speckled Hen, with a weekly guest real ale. Open: Monday to Saturday – 11am to 3pm and 6pm to 11pm; 12 to 3pm and 7pm to 10.30pm on Sundays. Frequently stays open longer on Saturdays and Bank Holidays if the weather and trade is good. Phone: (01507) 600750

Little Cawthorpe

A little gem that seems to have a protective fold of land around it. There is a village pond and a church, although neither is particularly impressive. The former looks as if a major takeover by weed seems imminent, yet the spring bubbles forth in this pond and creates the stream, the Long Eau. Part of this stream is also used as a road, for vehicles with a good ground clearance; the ford is not in any danger of being bridged and the speed of flow, noticeable as you approach the Royal Oak (if not when you leave), accounts for the pub's nickname. The church has gained steps up from the road since I was here last, so I presume the congregation is growing. The manor house dates from 1673.

Part of the stream has a special name too. Where it is a sunken lane about 15 feet wide with steep sides and hedges, it was leapt on horseback in 1866 by one Doctor Trout, Mayor of Louth at the time. He won the wager and thus the honour in the name bestowed, Trout's Leap.

The Royal Oak, Little Cawthorpe

The Walk

Standing with your back to the pond and the church on your right (A), walk up the road to the left. Go up the hill and you will see that the road curves and starts to go down again. Ignore a footpath sign on the left; two grain silos appear on the right and at about the same place, an old windmill tower can be seen over to the right. It is domed and has windows round the flatter part. How does the owner paint this part?

Stay on the road a little further to a track on the right at (B), which takes you along an easy to follow grass track between two fields. Here you can take time to admire the all round view of woods, Wolds, and wide expanses of cultivation. At the end of the first section there are left and right kinks in the path, and then you can aim at the right-hand end of Haugham Wood (C), which goes off towards the left a few hundred yards in front of you.

Having got to the end of the wood, walk along its boundary on the other side. It winds a bit and dips and climbs, but there is a point where the land-owner has spent a great deal of time and money on fencing to persuade you to follow the sweeping semicircle you see in front of you, bringing you to the corner of the wood you can see on your right. Fortunately the OS map shows your right of way going to the right straight to that point. When you are there, walk to the left along its short straight `end', and then take a straight course across the field to the hedge on the far side.

Going along this section shows another face of Lincolnshire. Without self publicity, landowners, possibly assisted, are getting on with a big programme, which must stretch across the country, of forestry manage-ment. The example on the left has good planting patterns and a mix of decid-uous with a few conifers that will, if followed up with good cutting and replanting plans, keep quite a few generations supplied with good wood and a profit.

Walking across the field aim for (D), which is the right-hand one of the few trees spaced out on the far hedgerow. Cross the shallow dry ditch and follow the well marked pathway over the next field. The path is regularly sprayed to keep it clear for walkers. This is a good time to reflect that on a path like this, you would never believe that Lincolnshire was flat.

On the other side of that last field is a tractor track. Turn right and go along it, then turn left at the next junction. There is a pond at the corner, (E), fortu-nately fenced off because it is used as a spraying equipment cleaning point, so you would be well advised to keep children (and animals) away from it. At the next junction along this track (F), you should see the top of the church tower at Burwell. That is enough to confirm that a left turn is to be made here.

Now, with a good path to stride out upon, keep the line as the tractor track runs out and go for the gap in the wood ahead. You will find that it confronts you with a grass slope to go down (G), then a short climb out of the other side. At the top is a track.

Cross the track, go through the gap and walk down the side of the wood on your left for a short distance. Over the next stile into a grass field, go down the right-hand side of it to another stile and pass a white farm house at (H); go down a short stretch of green lane, through the farmyard and left onto the metalled road at the hamlet of Muckton. When the road turns left after a short distance, go right down a farm lane. After Low Farm, turn left along a green lane (J) that runs parallel to the track of the dismantled railway.

The green lane cuts through a corner of Legbourne Wood and then curves around and along its right-hand side, so that when you cross the old railway bed again there is a lane in front that takes you back to Cawthorpe. Along

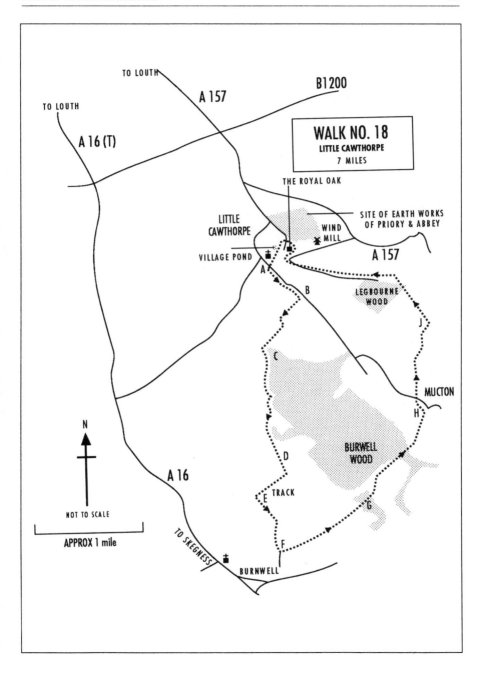

here there is the chance of a closer look at the windmill. When you get to the end of this road, turn right and at the water, go to the footpath at the right-hand side as it gets deeper later on. It is a chance to clean your wellies. Next, wade through the ford, go left and left again, into the Royal Oak. The road to the left leads through part of the village, past the pond and up to the church and you cannot be far from your vehicle.

The church at Little Cawthorpe

19. Horsington

Route: Horsington – Firgrove Farm – Old Woodhall – Poolham Hall – Horsington.

Pleasant and level walking.

Distance: 5 miles.

Start: North end of village at the Elder Tree. OS Landranger Series Map 122, square 1968.

Getting there: At Woodhall Spa, 6 miles from Bardney on the B1190. From Woodhall Spa, take the B1191 towards Horncastle, turn left at Martin Moor (2 miles from Woodhall cross-roads), a right and left close together at Reeds Beck Farm, then next left and the right turn after that (total 6 miles).

The Elder Tree

A pub for locals that I think would suit many visitors. The landlord works on the basis that John Smiths hand drawn together with Batesons is a formula too popular to need changing. The landlady takes note of the favourites on every menu that she makes as a sound base and adds new dishes occasionally to test reaction. I cannot say whether it is as good as it sounds, but the beer was very enjoyable.

Open Monday – Thursday 12am – 3pm, Friday – Saturday 11am – 3pm, evenings 6 – 11pm; usual Sunday hours. Phone: (01526) 388223

Horsington

Small and quiet, with one or two small businesses, Horsington seems typical of the small communities below the Wolds in central Lincolnshire, providing a walk that is an equally good example.

The Walk

Come out of the pub car park and turn right, follow the road round to the left past the church, and carry on to the next bend to the right. At that point, go to the left and at a white gateway (B) go into a farm stockyard / tractor sheds; by turning left past a Dutch barn with part of the roof coming off, go straight out the other side to cross the field.

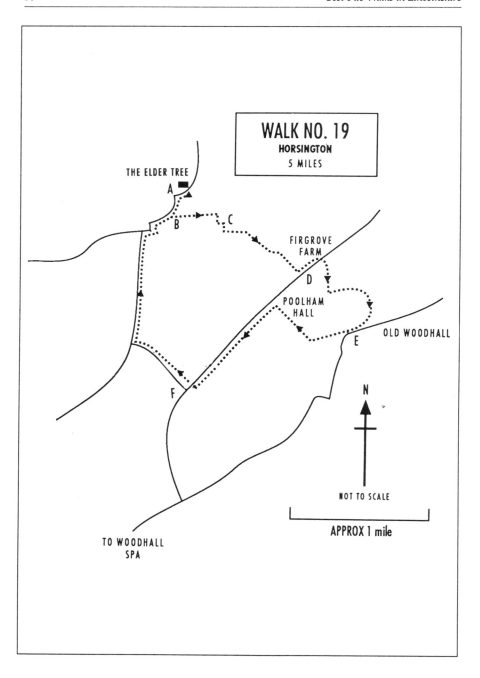

WALK NO. 19
HORSINGTON
5 MILES

THE ELDER TREE
A

B   C

FIRGROVE
FARM

D

POOLHAM
HALL

OLD WOODHALL

E

F

N

NOT TO SCALE

APPROX 1 mile

TO WOODHALL
SPA

After that there is a left and right turn at (C), but the tractor track stays with you and continues to point in the right direction. Although an old footpath sign is still there, it would be difficult to pick your way across the middle of a large field in such flat country, so use the tractor track until the road is reached at (D).

Turn left and at Firgrove Farm, the next on the right, use the farm road to go around the buildings to the right, and then walk along the field boundary with the hedge on your right. Cross the bridge over the drain and go straight up the side. When the drain starts to curve away from you to the left, follow it right around the field, finishing alongside the spinney (E). Go to the gate at the corner, carrying on through into the pasture. Walk to the right-hand end of the field and through a gate with rails on the dyke side and bear right to reach, at the end of the track, Poolham Hall. Turn left and walk along this minor road for half a mile.

At the white signpost (F), take the road indicated on the right. At certain times of the year it looks as if there is a path across the corner of the field and, though used by locals, it is not a designated footpath so try to ignore it.

It is now a mile along the road back to the pub. As you turn towards the village, there is a parallel path behind Mapleton Farm, but that bit of meandering could lose you the chance to see a couple of Model A Fords that occasionally run down this road from a garage near to the junction. All you can do now is make your way past a row of uniform bungalows on the left to the Elder Tree.

20. Corby Glen

Route: Corby Glen – Borton le Coggles – Corby Glen

The walk is easy and any blocked paths are bypassed.

Distance: 4½ miles.

Start: At parking area in village square. OS Landranger Series Map 130, square 9924.

Getting there: Corby Glen is about halfway between the A1 and Bourne on the A151.

The Fighting Cocks

There are a number of pubs in Corby Glen, making accommodation easier, but it is less easy to choose a pub. My favourite, the Fighting Cocks, is right in the centre, has a lot of character, and serves quite a few of them. The landlord is a pleasant sort, but by no means effusive, who serves a decent pint of hand pulled Tetleys, Bass, Worthington and Kilkenny. Food and a selection of wines are served every day from a varied menu. In 1999, this was changed regularly, but had popular stand-bys such as 8oz rump steaks at £6.50 and "specials" from £3.50. Phone: (01476) 550217

Corby Glen

At least one complete book has been written about this village. The fact is that it seems so cut off makes you wonder how it came to achieve its present size. Historical facts make it seem possible that the village has held together through some strong sense of community spirit. The market cross and annual sheep fair remind you that this has been a commercial centre since the thirteenth century. Unfortunately the new school building, on what seems to be a less than practical site, seems far less in keeping with the village and manor house than the old grammar school, now used for exhibitions. I have a good idea how the Prince of Wales would describe the new school.

The `Glen' bit of the name comes from the river that flows down the east side and starts to the north.

The Walk

From the market place go north (right if you are facing the Fighting Cocks), passing the Glaziers, another pub worth trying, then the Carmelite convent. Keep following the road and at the right-hand bend, look out for a large chestnut tree in the garden of a rustic red brick house with dormer windows. Opposite this house, there is an opening into the second `yard' from the corner, so cross the road at (A).

Go into the yard, which has cottages along both sides, and walk up to the top where the end of the white fronted cottage juts out. Go left of this, across the open land which looks like a builder's yard, to the wooden gate. Walk to the top right-hand corner of the field and go through the gate to continue walking over the pasture, Again, the stile you want is in the top right-hand corner (B) and because the stile is angled, turn 90 degrees after you have crossed it, to look across the field. Now look for the pylon just over the hedge at the far side. There is one to the left behind the trees and there is one to the right in the middle of the trees, but walk towards the central one, until you are halfway across. After that the path changes direction slightly to the left.

Now go for the gap between two pylons on the left. Once through the gap, go straight across the middle of the field. At this point, while heading towards a farm road, the path passes a spinney that seems insignificant in size and age, so I was surprised to see around twenty muntjak deer pour out of the far end and cross the field to the front and left.

At the hedge and gap you find a deep ditch with no bridge, but by going carefully down the side, it is not difficult to stride across the water and scramble up the other side. Another ditch, shortly after, is easier. From there, still striding across the field, aim for the last tree down the row from the farmhouse. Halfway across the field, change direction a little so that you are going towards the church spire on the far horizon. Join the farm road and turn right. At an obvious post, until now hidden by the brow of the hill, you will find a bridge fit for tractors over this last ditch onto the farm road. Turn left to the road at (C), and left again onto the B1176. At this turning I thought that even electricity pylons can look good; it is time for them to be considered part of the countryside.

Half a mile will bring you to a stile on the right at (D) four steps down from the road. Once over, go left at a bit of an angle and into the field. Go down this field alongside the fence on the right, to a substantial looking bridge that will take you over what appears to be a big ditch, but which undoubtedly is the River Glen. From the end of the bridge, cross the track to the hedge which

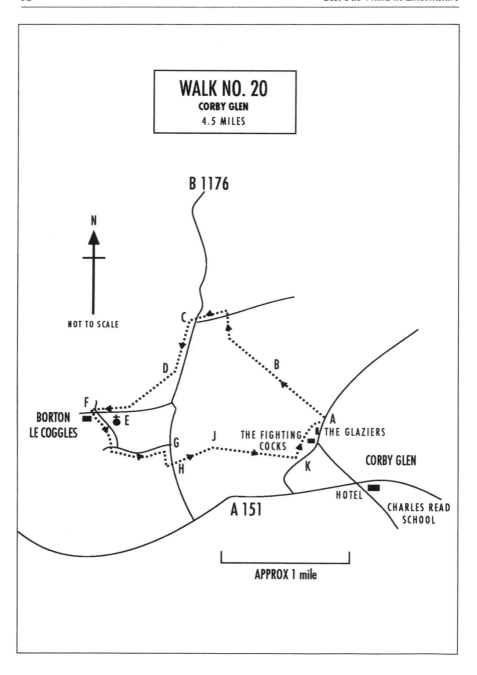

WALK NO. 20
CORBY GLEN
4.5 MILES

B 1176

N

NOT TO SCALE

C

D

B

F

BORTON
LE COGGLES

E

G   J   THE FIGHTING
COCKS

A
THE GLAZIERS

H

K

CORBY GLEN

HOTEL

A 151

CHARLES READ
SCHOOL

APPROX 1 mile

is to the left in front of you, and go up, under the tree, continuing upwards with the hedge on your left.

In this gently rolling sort of country, we tend to stop less to look round than on a steeper hill. Here is a good place to put that right. Stop and look now and again near the top at the woodland, fields, hedges, trees and streams, not to mention the sheer peacefulness unless an Intercity 125 goes by.

From here the path, according to the Ordnance Survey map, goes from here to the church ahead. Unfortunately a stream that is too wide to jump is in the way, so go downstream (left) a bit to a bridge of sorts, then you can head for the church, over the stile at (E) and right into the road. Opposite the church is the rectory, a splendid old house, and further along, the Hare and Hounds at the junction, which regretfully does not appear to open at lunchtime. Go past it down the road which goes left at the junction, allowing you to see a little more of Burton le Coggles. The road will also bring you down to the B1176 again at (G).

From (G) to the point where the path head across the fields again is only about 200 yards, so don't miss it. On the left, by the dead oak held together by ivy, the pointer at (H) directs you down into the valley, over the stile (mind the electric fencing wire strung overhead). From there you can see the bridge (J) that has to be crossed, as the new wood is obvious and the stakes at each end have white paint on them. Bidding farewell to the Glen, head for the hedge in front of you and walk alongside it to the right. You need to climb another stile and cross another grass field, then go between the houses out onto a minor road. Go left up to that red brick house again, turning right to go down the main road and back to the Fighting Cocks.

21. Horncastle

Route: Horncastle – Langton – Thimbleby – Horncastle

An easy walk with a good choice of pubs.

Distance: 4 ½ miles.

Start: From B1191, take the second side road on the left after leaving the A158 traffic lights. This lane has a public footpath sign at its entrance. Cars can be driven down and parked on the left just after a large warehouse. OS Landranger Series Map 122, square 2569.

Getting there: Horncastle is served by A roads that approach from four directions. The B1191 is the first road on the left after passing the church heading north on the A158(T).

Pubs

As this is the only walk to start from a town of any size, it is impractical to give a guide to all of the good pubs in town. Two of the many with a good

The Angel Inn

name are the Kings Head, the Batemans pub with the thatched roof, and the Angel, a free house opposite the entrance to the hospital. Also noticeable on entering the town are the Fighting Cocks, the Crown, a free house, the Bull Hotel, the Admiral Rodney, Old Nicks, the Ship and quite a few others. Phone: (01507) 522214

Horncastle

This is a pleasant place between the Wolds and the Fens that was a walled town in Roman times and a key point in the Civil War. It was near here, as battles raged to and fro, that the final throw of the dice went in Cromwell's favour. Other items of historical interest range from sections of Roman wall to almost modern contemporary times. It was here that Alfred, Lord Tennyson met Emily for only the second time at a friend's wedding; he became engaged to marry her four or five years later, after success with his poetry made marriage financially possible.

The Walk

From the parking area (A), walk down to the end of the lane where a sign directs you along a path between a bungalow and a hedge. Follow the left-hand route that goes between the hedge and a wire fence. Cross over the ditch at the end of the field and go slightly to the right as indicated by the waymark. This will bring you to another bridge over a ditch about 20 yards down the wire fence. Once over that, go diagonally over the field to the right to the far hedge and bottom corner (B). Here there is another bridge and a pointer that sends you across the next field towards a group of six or seven small trees at the far hedge (C); go through the gap and left on B1911.

From this corner, there is a little over half a mile to walk to Thornton. Although only a B road, it is occasionally busy, so take care. It is not difficult to let your attention wander as the view, especially on the left, is a good one. Go left at the next road junction, then curve right with the road.

At the edge of Thornton, from the next house, there is a footpath on the right-hand side of the road, which is a help. Pass the telephone box, then the entrance to the vicarage (where the path stops) and take the lane on the right at (D). This leads you up to a house and round its left-hand side. After that you are on a good grass track.

There is a ditch on your right now; I found a scarecrow here with a short length of pipe, to look like a man with a gun. The crop of peas seemed to be

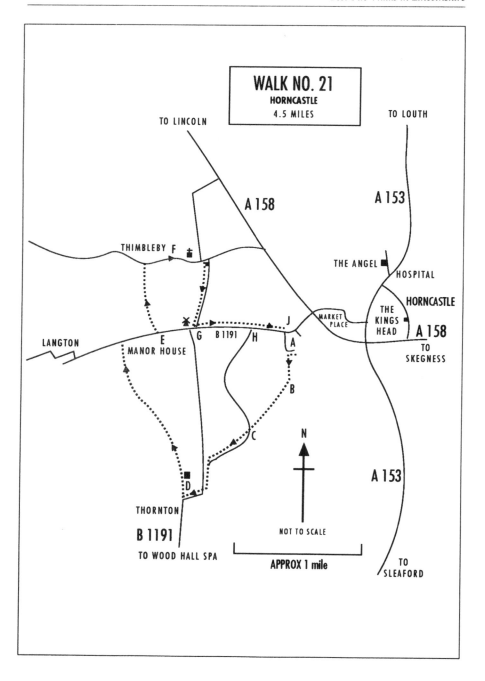

coming on well. Keep following the grass track as it comes to the wood and then goes down the left-hand side. At the end of the wood, turn to the left, and when you come to a gate go through and turn right. Approaching the farm, take the path to the left of the black barn, at the end of which a short path takes you past the houses on the left and then down onto the road.

Turn right here. This is Langton, which has a few nice houses and on your right, the well kept and efficient looking Manor House Farm. Soon after that there is a path that starts on your left after the cottage with the corrugated iron roof. The stile is practically on the bend and starts the path that goes straight to the village you can see ahead. Ignore a stump over to your left with a waymark, and aim at the corner you can see ahead where there is a bridge to cross the drain and a marker post. At the opposite side of the next field there are farm buildings to the right, and a row of houses on the left lining the road; you turn right here. The path takes in Thimbleby by turning left at (E) because it is a pleasant example of a Lincolnshire village which seems to look purpose built to form `typical' village. At (F) is an example of what is happening to villages like this, a community post office. I was told that local people are trying to keep the village alive with various activities and regard a working post office as a necessity. In this case it can only be done on a part-time basis, opening only on Tuesday mornings and Thursday afternoons. I can only admire the effort, but wonder at the same time what is the point of Lindsey County Council declaring the eastern part of this village a conservation area, if it means that there cannot be any new blood at the essential levels to restore life to the place.

At the end of the road is the church and a right and left turn. Walk along the left-hand side of the road until you come to the Durham Ox. Turn right and walk down towards the remaining tower of the windmill. Along this road you will notice more hedges and wooded areas, with consequent increase in birdsong, than in the surrounding countryside. Even more obvious are the well kept gardens, many with flowering trees such as cherry.

At the road junction (G), turn left and walk towards the outskirts of Horncastle. For about half a mile the road stays fairly high above the plain in front of you, giving wonderful views over the town and its surroundings. After that it goes down quite quickly, before coming to the lane on the right (H) from which the walk started. Either before or after you pick up your car, I recommend a stroll into Horncastle, taking the road the other side of the A158 past the old market place, which held the biggest horse fairs in the country until near the end of the last century. From there, you will find many small shops and convenient hostelries.

22. Mareham-le-Fen

Route: Mareham – Enderby Hill – Toft Grange – Bridge House – towards Grange Farm – Mareham

Twists and turns, but easy walking. Waymarks peter out towards end of walk.

Distance: 5½ miles.

Start: At the cross roads adjacent to the Royal Oak. OS Landranger Series Map 122, square 2761.

Getting there: Mareham is on the A155 between Coningsby and East Keal.

The Royal Oak

This charming whitewashed, thatched inn, one of the oldest thatched pubs in England, next to the crossroads is pretty, has a good landlord and good beer. In an area where walkers tend to think of farmers as hostile, it is ex-

The Royal Oak

traordinary that three landlords in this area, out of the five in the whole county, volunteered that should I or my friends let them know we are coming in a group, at any hour, drinks and/or a meal can be made ready at any time. Meals can be ordered at the start of your walk to be ready when you say you will return. In good weather, the Royal Oak is likely to stay open all day anyway. More power to the landlord's elbow. Phone: (01507)568357

Mareham-le-Fen

This small village, with a busy main road, has restored medieval church, with a fourteenth-century tower.

The Walk

From the crossroads, go north away from the A155 and take the first lane to the right, just after the monkey puzzle tree. This is Church Lane, which quickly changes in width to just a path and then proceeds to lead you around the church and church yard. When the road is reached, turn left, and at the following junction, right. The route now goes through a smart looking neighbourhood before reaching the entrance to a farm and buildings on the left. Go straight through the yard and through the field at the other side of the yard at (B), going along the same line as the power cables. When the hedge across the front is reached, turn to the left and carry on until the footpath sign and gap are reached.

The path comes out just where there is a bend at (C) and carries on to the right as far as Enderby Hall Farm. At that junction of roads and farm lanes, turn left and carry on along the track marked Toft Grange, through really open country. Here I was treated to a spectacular display by Tornado fighter bombers, which made me miss the turning on the left. In fact, the sign is easy to see and is about yards before the entrance to Toft Grange Farm. Here starts a well defined grass path that leads to a bridge and another clear path across the centre of the next field. When this runs out onto a cart track, go left and then right and onto the road at (D), past Railway Cottage and Scotts Fruits. Here the route is to the left down a secondary road until you arrive at the A155. Go along to the left for few yards and cross over with great care to the track that leads into the fields opposite, where some old machinery has been dumped at (E). Our path crosses what is approaching fenland, following a drain on your right. At one point, a sharp right takes you over a wide bridge, the path continues for a few yards, goes left again and resumes a southerly

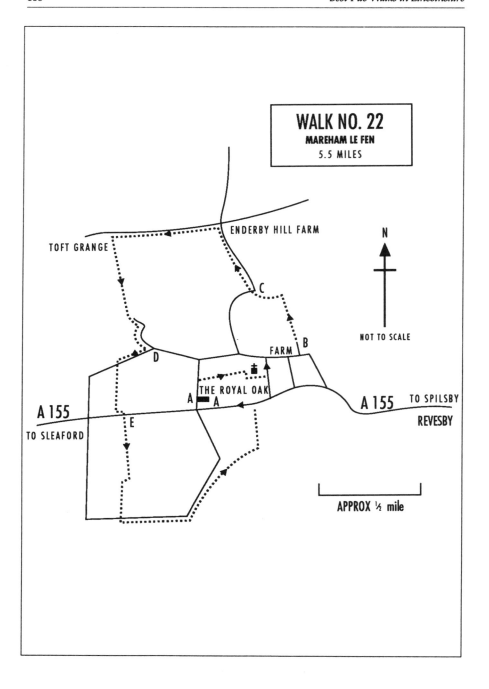

course. This one is straight and true, right down to the road, where you turn left.

A sign pointing left saying `New York 4 miles' will give everyone the chance to make jokes about how much money they have saved by buying this book instead of flying Concorde. However, we ignore it and walk on, taking the left-hand bend in the road and walking along an almost parallel track to the large drain on the right.

When the drain bends away to the right and you can see along the left-hand bank, go into the field, cross over to the bank and walk alongside it. Plenty of ducks will keep you company along this bit. When you come to the bridge, go left instead of crossing it. This means walking with a smaller drain on your right until you reach the cart track at the top. Go left just far enough to cross the drain to your left. Once into the field, go left along the edge until you come to the minor drain, where you turn right and head for the tower of Wainfleet All Saints church.

At the low white cottage that confronts you as you come up the field, go round the left-hand side, either by struggling through a minor gap near the cottage or going a bit further to a gap and walking back along the other side of the hedge. Either way, you should pass along the rear of the house to scramble over a small ditch at the end, so that you can turn right to maintain course for the tower. The drain now on your left will turn left and then meet another ditch or drain. Follow them with a left and right turn. A Peugeot dealer's yard now confronts you. Go to the right, around the bungalow and come to the main road. All you have to do now is keep on walking along the road to our left to the Royal Oak.

23. Horbling

Route: Horbling – Stow Farm – Threekingham – Holland Road Farms – Horbling

Flat and easy; worth the walk as seeing two villages is a bonus.

Distance: 5 miles.

Start: Opposite the church. OS Landranger Series Map 130, square 1135.

Getting there: Horbling is just off the Grantham to Boston road, on the B1394 or the B1177.

The Plough

This a free house which is just off the village main street, nearly opposite the church. The present landlord and his family took over in September 1993 and have completely restored the place, ensuring that it remained a typical country village pub, modernising but without spoiling the overall picture. If you see the wooden beams, floors plus the open fires for yourself, you will agree that nothing has been added to create the brewery design office `theme'. Even the snug, with only eight seats, remains as a popular room which has, I am told, occasionally held over 20. Food is available lunchtime and evening and ranges from a quick snack to lunch or dinner.

Beers: Boddingtons and Old Speckled Hen plus a different guest ale every week. Open Monday – Saturday 11am – 3pm, 6.30 – 11pm; usual Sunday hours. Phone: (01529) 240263

Horbling

This is an attractive village with some lovely old cottages, a stream, big old chestnut trees and a cross shaped church, but (unfairly) is overshadowed by the alleged history of its neighbour, Threekington.

In the latter's case, it was the Lord of Bourne who, in 870, reckoned he had had enough of the terrorising Danes. With the help of a raised force, he proceeded to kill three Danish kings. This is, at least, one of the stories about how the village got its name. Up on the main road, there is a Three Kings Inn, where previous guests have been King John, Henry VIII and Dick Turpin.

By the gate of the old Hall stand the two jawbones of a whale. Apparently, this manor house on Laundon Road had belonged to the Cragg family for generations, who owned most of the land hereabouts. One particular member of the family, a Captain Cragg, chased whales in the way others around here chased foxes, only more profitably for a while. He then apparently overextended himself, by putting everything into a bigger ship; when it sank, he lost everything except the whale jawbones. I could not imagine someone who has to leap for his life tucking a couple of whalebones into his waistcoat pocket, but this story was the nearest I could get to the reason for such an unusual archway to the drive of a manor house in Lincolnshire.

The Walk

Start at the church, cross the road and go down the lane there, passing the Plough. Turn the corner to the right and opposite the pub car park take the short green lane which goes between a house and a wall. Go over the stile and keep a straight line over the next field until you come to a stile in the far left-hand corner. Step over it and turn left on the old railway track. As this gets a bit boggy, climb up the embankment to the right and go left to where the old railway bridge is protected by Armco. At (B), start walking to your right along the road for about three quarters of a mile to the entrance to Stow Farm (C).

On the right-hand side of the road there is the entrance to a field that has a decent headland to walk down with the hedge on your left, until at the bottom you come to a large pond (D). By initially going right and then left you can get around the pond quite easily. Walk up to the large single tree at the bottom corner of the grass field on your left and then start to walk along the side of the drain, ditch or stream until you come to the road. The marked path on the OS map takes a diagonal line across the field, but walking across plough is no fun. Once on the road, you will find a vandalised footpath marker post.

Further along, on the left, a footpath pointer indicates a path that looks as if it should head for the right-hand far corner of the field, but it is not easy to see where any such path might end. So walk to the right along the edge of the field and then straight across to the left-hand end of the yard ahead, which looks like a combination of tyre scrapyard, tin recovery plant and anything else mechanical. Walk along and around the perimeter and turn right down the lane at the far side. The public footpath sign points this way and if anything, points across the yard rather than around it. On the road proper, take the first right and then, when below the church, go up the footpath on the left to the churchyard.

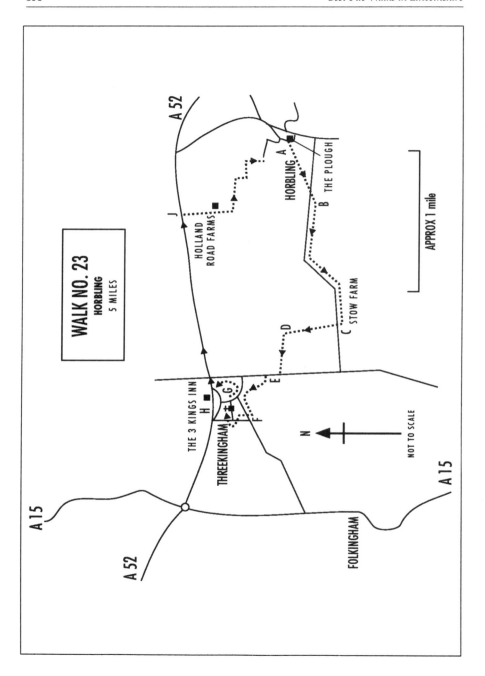

WALK NO. 23
HORBLING
5 MILES

A 52

A 15

A 52

A 15

HORBLING

B THE PLOUGH

A

HOLLAND
ROAD FARMS

J

C STOW FARM

D

E

F

G

H

THE 3 KINGS INN

THREEKINGHAM

FOLKINGHAM

N

NOT TO SCALE

APPROX 1 mile

Go out onto a curved road, right and then right again to the gates of the hall for a quick look at the whalebones, then back up to the Three Kings Inn. Depending on the hour and the weather, go as soon as convenient along the road to the right and the A52. It is a busy road but the verge is wide. The snag about fenland walking is that if someone has blocked a path in any way, the drainage system ensures that you have a long way to go to an alternative. Strictly speaking, the fens are on the other side of Horbling but it is best not to take too many risks.

One mile down the road at (J), Holland Road Farms has a clearly defined path that goes away to the right. Go through the immaculate gravelled entrance, the one-time stack yard and present-day machinery park and out along the tractor track. Go straight up towards the not too distant horizon on the brow of the hill in front of you. From here it is bridge, gateway bridge, over a ditch, past a brick building on your left until at the top a small plantation is found; here go to the left-hand side of the hedge. After the plantation, go for the next gap on your right and from that point, turn and walk diagonally across the field on the left, aiming at first for a point that is about two-thirds to three-quarters along the bottom hedge. As you get closer you will see that the point you are heading towards is just to the right of the church tower. Now walk to the far end of the field along that second hedge to get onto the old railway embankment (K), and go to the right. A bit further on, the way is blocked by high brambles, so go down the left-hand side on to the edge of the field and turn right. At the end of the field, take the farm track that goes to the left and follow it down to the road junction and a white bungalow. Turn left to the village street and there turn right, passing a large house which has been converted into solicitors' offices and which has an old fire insurance badge on the wall, dated 1716. A little bit further on are the Plough Inn and the church.

24. Caythorpe

Route: Caythorpe – Frieston – Hough on the Hill – Caythorpe.

Easy walking. Care needed with directions.

Distance: 5½ miles.

Start: At the road junction opposite the church. OS Landranger Series Map 130, square 9348.

Getting there: Take the A17 east from the A1 near Newark, turning right after about 3 miles into Caythorpe

The Pubs

This lucky village has two good pubs to cater for all tastes. The Wagon and Horses is possibly the best pub to choose during the day as it seems to attract more local custom and has the best atmosphere. It is a Mansfields house, but serves a good pint just the same. There are also lagers and Guinness.

The **Red Lion** is a free house that dates from the seventeenth century. Meals are served lunchtime and evening in the bar and restaurant and the beers are Boddingtons, Bass, Wadsworths 6X plus a guest ale. Prince Charles, it is said, used the pub as his local when he was at Cranwell.

The **Wagon and Horses** is open Monday – Saturday 12am – 3pm, 7 – 11pm. Food served every day except Sunday and Monday. Red Lion open 11am – 3pm, 6 – 11pm; usual Sunday restrictions.Phone (Wagon and Horses): (01400) 272365

Caythorpe

A sizeble place off the Lincoln to Grantham road, Caythorpe has a nine-teenth-century hall with reputedly the oldest mulberry tree in England. There is also an agricultural college at Caythorpe Court. The village also boasted an iron foundry until not long ago, down near the old station. Now the only industry seems, apart from farming, to be a copper cylinder and boiler making company. It is a very pleasant village, which I have earmarked for a more leisurely visit.

The Walk

Coming out of the High Street at the church (D), turn right onto what is the old Lincoln Road and go up to the main road, the A607, to turn right again. The football field is on this corner to your right and has a good level looking cricket square, although the boundaries look a bit short on two sides. A few yards up the road there is a footpath sign on either side of the road, just by the end of that sports field. Cross the road to go left over the stile in the hedge at (E).

From here there is a choice of routes. The easy way is to go straight up the field until you come to a spoil heap on the left as the field ends. This takes you up to the site of the old station. Go round the end of the red brick building and then, opposite the middle of the building, walk across the middle of the next field. Aim towards the clump of trees, at which point you will see a hedge that runs ahead of you. Follow the path by keeping the ditch and hedge on your right to (H). Alternatively, if it is excessively muddy or the crops are at a stage that makes you want to avoid walking through them, go to the left, join the road at (F) and turn right to go over the old railway bridge. Ignore the first entry in the fields on your right, go past the hedge that goes away at a right angle, and then as power lines go overhead turn right where there are two sleepers over the ditch (G) and onto a path which goes straight to a corner, jutting out towards you at (H).

Walk straight on to the next field corner and turn half right through the spinney (where there are usually three or four varieties of butterfly during the warmer parts of the year). At the end of the spinney turn half right again so that a ditch is on the left, follow the path heading 100 yards or so to the point where the ditch stops, then go ahead, across the field to a group of three or four smallish trees. At that point, turn left (without going through the gate) and walk along the side of the hedge that is now on your right. At the end of that stretch there is a sharp right-hand turn; continue along the field boundary, with the hedge still on the right, until the track of the old railway line is reached.

When you have crossed this, go along the boundary to the power line poles and turn left: do not follow the line of the poles, but aim for a point about 15 yards to the right of some white fencing at the far side of the field. A footpath sign will be found there, next to a small bridge across the ditch. Go over that and onto the road, turn right and recross the A607. This is Frieston, where you need to take the road slightly to the right as you cross. Follow its curves until you reach the green, where there at least a couple of decent look-

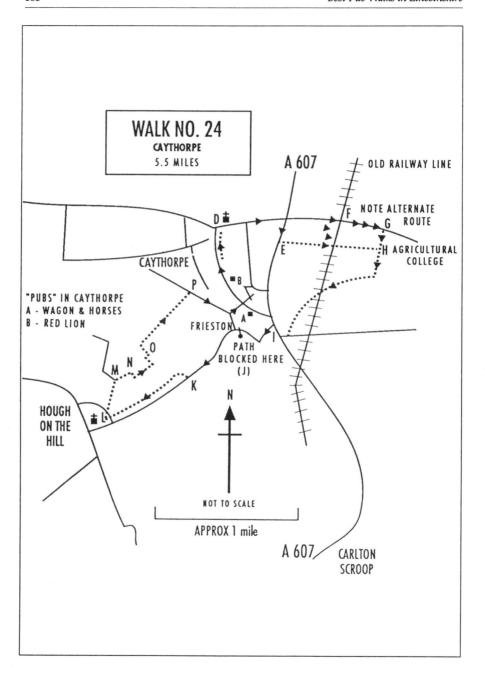

WALK NO. 24
CAYTHORPE
5.5 MILES

A 607

OLD RAILWAY LINE

NOTE ALTERNATE ROUTE

F

G

D

E

H AGRICULTURAL COLLEGE

CAYTHORPE

P

B

"PUBS" IN CAYTHORPE
A - WAGON & HORSES
B - RED LION

FRIESTON

A

I

O

PATH BLOCKED HERE (J)

M N

K

HOUGH ON THE HILL

L

N

NOT TO SCALE

APPROX 1 mile

A 607 CARLTON SCROOP

ing houses. Walk to the end of the green, ignoring a road that goes back to Caythorpe, and carry on towards Hough on the Hill.

House on the Green at Frieston

Author's Note

In the first edition of this book, when describing a possible extension to this walk, I had to point out that the path going south from Frieston was blocked at the road side. We are told now (April 1999) that the householders have kept the path open for at least the past two years. Unfortunately, it cannot continue straight across to the road running east to west to Hough on the Hill because the lakes are, in fact, quarries that have filled with water and any earlier ridge has disappeared. It is, however, possible to walk around them, as long as you stay as close to the original path as possible, but that does make it a much longer walk.

Lincolnshire Highways Department have told me that they did negotiate another route with the landowner, only to have a local walking group raise objections, apparently because it would have meant a walk of 100 yds along the main road. If any future negotiations fail to please all parties, it will go to a public meeting – a course of action which has seen paths in similar circumstances being closed completely.

When a house on the left is reached (K) opposite sheds and paddocks, a track goes up a slight incline to the right. By following this, a path is joined at the top, going to the left. From here it is fairly easy going as the church tower is in front of you and makes a convenient aiming point. Crossing the middle of a field, after a tractor track, go over a stile and aim for the right-hand end of the right-hand barn where there is a gate. Now veer slightly right to another stile at the other side of the field, then follow the line of trees on your left to the stile that lets you out into the lane at (L). Go along the lane to the right and down the right-hand track at the junction.

Walking between hedgerows from (L) to (M), you can take the first path that goes to the right by going through a double gate and heading for the far left-hand corner and another double metal gate that lets you out onto the track you were following, but saving a few yards. So turn right and then go straight on at the junction of the bridleways (M). At (N) the track seems to peter out, but by turning right along the field dividing strip, after passing the end of the drain that goes along to your right, you can go around the boundary of two fields: turn left at the first corner, walk along beside the hedge to the next corner, turn left again, walk along this boundary, and look for a reasonable place to get into the field on your right.

This done, go to the hedge, turn right so that the hedge is on your left and stride out until you reach a significant track. Upon this turn right. You will soon come to the village, pass the Woodyard on Chapel Lane, see the church pop out from behind the buildings and arrive at High Streetby the Wagon and Horses.

The walking here is easy but was found to be frustrating on my last visit, due to some unhelpful land owners. This may change.

25. Oasby

Route: Oasby – Aisby – Aunsby – Culverthorpe – Oasby

Gently rollimg countryside which opens up new vistas throughout the walk.

Distance: 8 miles.

Start: The Houblon Arms. OS Landranger Series Map 130, square 0039.

Getting there: Follow the A52 GranthamBoston road for about 8 miles before turning left for Oasby.

The Houblon Arms

This is one of those gems that walkers are always hoping they may stumble upon, and later in the day wish they lived a bit closer. The exterior is attractive, the interior a good starting point for the landlord and his wife to impose some atmosphere, and there is good food too. Accommodation is available at the Houblon Arms and at Wayside Cottage, (01529) 455246. Beers: Bass, Batemans and guest beers. Again, it is said that Prince Charles was a regular customer when he was at Cranwell. Open 12am – 3pm, 6 – 11pm and the usual Sunday restrictions. Phone: (01529)455215

The Houblon Arms

Oasby

Somehow or other, nearly all Oasby's buildings have managed to be in keeping with whatever was here before. The Inn is picturesque, there is a Manor House with a cedar, and sufficient byways to puzzle a stranger for half a day's walking, partly due perhaps to the fact that they all seem to curve and a few are sunken. It is also quite impressive to find that every garden is carefully tended.

The Walk

On leaving the Houblon Arms, turn to the left, pass the village shop and then look out for the sign on the left-hand side at the corner (B). Go where it points, alongside the house on your right, curving around between two hedges before going into a field. Keep to that line until a single storey house on your right is passed and then turn right. When you meet the road, go left a couple of paces before turning right to go down the right-hand side of the football field. As you reach the road again a new house with very high, steep roofing appears. The garage is the same and makes use of the space, judging by the windows, but I wonder why the house roof was built like that?

To go through this little hamlet, follow the road marked 'No Through Road' so that you pass the phone box and the rest of the village hiding behind that sign.

After passing Sycamore House and a very impressive farmhouse, the tarmac road gives up the ghost. The track is quite good: it curves to the right and then makes an extended zig-zag, left, right, left before coming to a turn about a mile from the hamlet, going to the left at a right angle. It is not difficult to miss this: if you arrive at a T-junction, turn round and go back to the proper point (D).

Carry on until you reach the road at (E), Dembleby. Turn left and follow the road to a junction, where you turn right to Aunsby. Aunsby is a pleasant diversion down a country lane that ends with a small group of houses, a church and a farm. After the church and one more house on your right, there is a drive up to the farm on your left. The path starts at a stile to the right of the farm drive entrance and goes diagonally across the field passing near to the right of the farm buildings. Should there be any reason to be hesitant about this, perhaps mares and very young foals in the field, the farmer won't mind you going round by his yard, preferably finding him to explain first.

By one way or another, you will arrive at the gate of the drive at the other side of the farm. Here, on the road, turn sharp left and head for the gap in the

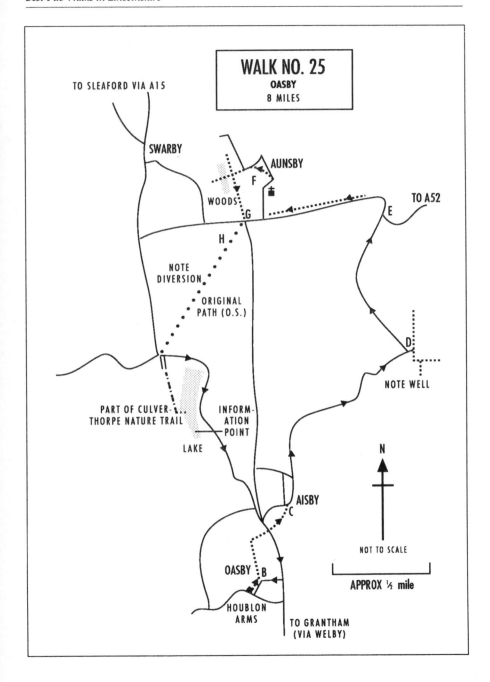

WALK NO. 25
OASBY
8 MILES

TO SLEAFORD VIA A15

SWARBY

AUNSBY

F

WOODS

G

TO A52

E

H

NOTE
DIVERSION

ORIGINAL
PATH (O.S.)

D

NOTE WELL

PART OF CULVER-
THORPE NATURE TRAIL

INFORM-
ATION
POINT

LAKE

N

NOT TO SCALE

AISBY

C

APPROX ½ mile

OASBY   B

HOUBLON
ARMS

TO GRANTHAM
(VIA WELBY)

middle of the wood in front of you. When you get there, cross the substantial looking footbridge and turn left to walk with the wood on your right. This takes you to (G), a road junction that has a road to Oasby straight ahead and the footpath bisecting the right-hand corner. Take this path, which goes straight, according to the OS map, for 300 yards or so and then comes to a new marker. This explains why, on the map, a path is indicated as `original path'. The landowner has reached agreement with the local authorities quite recently that the route can go round the boundaries of his fields to avoid seasonal changes and possible arguments; every corner and turn is marked by a stout pole with waymark arrows. The extra distance is negligible and in fact something is added to the scenery. The path is clear, the edges of the field wide enough to walk along quite easily and the bridges and stiles in a good state of repair.

It eventually ends at the road, just a little way east of the junction at Culverthorpe. This path follows the road from here back to Oasby, as the road is quiet most days. Should you wish to walk an extra couple of miles or so, you can go back to the junction and on your left find the entrance that will let you join the nature trail laid out in the park. Part way back along the road you will be able to take a shorter diversion as the path follows a strip by the lake that will be seen very near to the road. One path goes along the lake edge and then, at the information and picnic point, another goes into the park.

The approach to Oasby is obvious, as you pass the first junction and then see the signpost at the second. Nearing the village pass a large, fairly new house is passed on the left-hand side, with paddocks, stables and such, a few well kept bungalows on the right; at a T-junction, make a right turn. Follow the twists and turns of this road and in a couple of minutes you are back at the Houblon Arms.

26. Huttoft

Route: Huttoft – Thurlby – Mumby – Anderby – Huttoft.

Easy – the twists and turns are not as confusing as they look!

Distance: 4½ miles.

Start: Near the Axe and Cleaver. OS Landranger Series Map 122, square 5176.

Getting there: On the A52, midway between Mablethorpe and Skegness.

The Axe and Cleaver

Despite its unusual name, this fairly modern pub is pleasant, roomy and reasonably comfortable. The landlord was welcoming and volunteered that he was always ready to open early or stay open for groups of walkers wanting food and drink, if they would give him a ring to let him know when they would be arriving. Home cooked fresh food is available and the ambience is enhanced with an open fire. Opening hours depend on the weather and the numbers of visitors during the summer.

Beers: Theakstones and I.P.A. Open all hours. Phone: (01507) 490205

The Axe and Cleaver

Huttoft

If you wonder how a village might spring up and exist in one part of the flat area along this coast, the map will tell you that here the land here is slightly higher; even two metres, allows a road to run not too far from the coast, and means a lot when you are nearly surrounded by salt marshes. The church has a thirteenth-century tower, and between the village and the coast there is evidence of a submerged prehistoric forest. More unusually, there used to be a custom at the village school that lasted until after World War I, of the boys locking the teacher out every year on the morning after Ash Wednesday. If they kept him out until midday they won the rest of the day as a holiday.

The Walk

Coming out of the pub car park, walk along the roadside to the left. A bungalow on the right has an unusual name, `Churns', which you will understand when you pass by. Shortly after `Chestnuts', cross the road to take the lane on the right, where the roadsign says Bilsby and Alford, and walk down past the church (B) to take the next lane on the left. At first it is metalled, but as it turns to go back to the main street, carry on along what is a farm track.

The path on the map goes across a field on your right but, as you might see, signs have been left on the gate to say `no shooting keep out' or `keep out bulls in field', so go to the end of this short lane to (C) and turn right to walk down the headland with the hedge on your right until you come to the drain at the bottom. Turn right and carry on over three gates until you cross the track of the dismantled railway, and then go with the drain as it bears left.

On reaching the road (D), walk along it to the left and then turn left again when it joins the next road, the B1449, with its sign to Mumby. There is a hill here: it is only the old railway bridge, but it does give the opportunity to see what a good job someone has made, converting the station house into a home. Life in these secluded hamlets was illustrated as I was passing the house and the milkman arrived, at quarter to two in the afternoon.

Turn right after the bridge and go for about a quarter of a mile, taking in a bend to the left, a more gentle one to the right, and a slight slope, passing on your left an enormous manure heap. This precedes the gap in the hedge at (E) which reveals the track you want to take. As you turn left onto this track a gap is clearly seen at the other side of the field, through which the path goes before turning right. From here, it is a straight half mile, cutting through farmland with only birdsong and the occasional distant tractor to be heard. I did not see any Tornado jets on this occasion, only one light aircraft that looked as if it was making for Ingoldmells, the airfield serving Skegness.

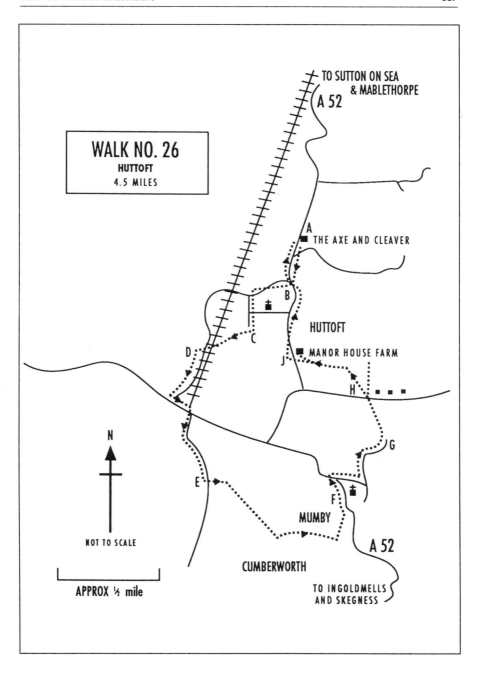

The green lane finally turns left by a lone Scots Pine and goes over a stout bridge to continue into the village of Mumby. Pass the farm buildings and the 30 mph limit signs and turn left at the road junction along Washdyke Lane. This takes you to the main road, where you turn left past the Red Lion (F). At a corner where the main road turns left, with a shop advertising snacks ahead of you, the lane you need to take is on your right. Walk down it to the triangle and then turn left. The road swings to the right just after a white bungalow and changes to an earth track with grass down the middle. Next you will see a brick built house on the left and, in front and to the right, a gate with a waymark on the right-hand side of it. When the stile has been crossed, keep along the hedge on your right until you come to a planked bridge at (G).

After that, either walk straight across the field towards the left-hand building on the road at the other side, or pick a tractor track to walk along that goes near to the same point, or go round the perimeter of the field to the right. There are two or three gaps in the hedge at the other side; the one to the left with a bit of fencing looks the safest. Cross the road and go left of the left-hand bungalow and into the field at (H). Again, you can choose either to go straight down the right-hand hedge, left at the bottom and back up a little way to cross the bridge; or to go diagonally across to the bridge about three-quarters of the way down the left-hand side of the field. The first is drier if the grass is wet, and the hedge is usually full of birds; the other is shorter.

In the end, the bridge is crossed despite the hawthorn, and the path is to the right. Turn left at the next ditch and walk up beside the fence to the road which is straight ahead at (J). You come out before Manor House Farm which you will pass after turning right. The remainder of the walk is through the village, passing the garage on the left which also appears to be an agency for a rather interesting electric commuter car. On the right there is a windmill tower with a lorry on top and a few yards further, The Axe and Cleaver.

27. Skendleby

Route: Skendleby – Dalby Hall – Langton – Partney – Skendleby.

Easy, but lacks waymarks below Thorp Farm. Follow the instructions!

Distance: 7 miles.

Start: Skendleby church (small parking area). OS Landranger Series Map 122, square 4369.

Getting there: Left off the A158, 1¾ miles from Partney roundabout. Partney is 2 miles north of Spilsby, 6 miles south of Alford and 11 miles west of Skegness.

The Blacksmiths Arms

On the main street in the village, this pub appears popular with walkers – an extra room seating thirty and a summer patio have been added. It sells Batemans beer, which I think is a fairly easily acquired taste. Three different bitters and a mild are on sale in the bar, a very small room that makes all conversations public (why do the most boring people in pubs always have the loudest voices?). There are other rooms however with an extension primarily for diners . The food is quite good and the service pleasant. Open 11.30 to 3pm and 7 to 11pm Monday to Friday, 11am to 11pm Saturday, usual Sunday hours. Phone: (01754) 890662

Skendleby

Claimed by many to be one of Lincolnshire's most charming villages, it certainly contains the right ingredients with a manor house, a hall, thatched cottages, a very villagey pub and a church with a cedar in the churchyard. Add to this a stream and the archaeological importance it gained when a barrow from c.1800BC was uncovered, and a lot of people will agree.

The Walk

Walk through the churchyard to the far right-hand corner, go through the gap, aim for the bottom corner of the field and go over a stile. Then comes a bit of fancy footwork to get around the boggy bits, onto some decent grass again and straight on up to the next stile. After that stile go along the bottom of the field to the next gate and stile by the corner of the wood (B). Once through that, make your way to the next gate in the far left-hand corner: to do this you will need to walk around another bit that gets a bit soft at times.

Avoid the temptation to go up to the farm on your right, as it would take you onto the road too far away from this line.

Continue along the edge of the field to the far end and then turn right. Go along this boundary until you can cross into the field on your left, to walk along with that hedge on your left. Turn right at the bottom once again and walk past the fence with a stile. Instead, cross the ditch ahead via the plank. From that plank and ditch, turn half right and head towards the halfway point of the wood running along the right-hand side, then go along the tractor path by turning left when you come up to the wood. The next gate takes you into the park of Dalby Hall, giving you a good view of the hall as you pass and finally come to the gates and then the road. Almost opposite at (C), just slightly to the left, is the path to take. Climb over the sort of stile and carry on down the field to the small gate at the bottom.

Dalby Hall

The next small gate is at the bottom left-hand corner. Go through it and over a bridge, and walk along with the hedge on your left. Keep going, and at the end of the farm track turn left. You are now at Langton, and as you walk past the post box and then the phone box, you will see an unusual octagonal thatch roofed cottage on the right at (D), followed by America Farm on your

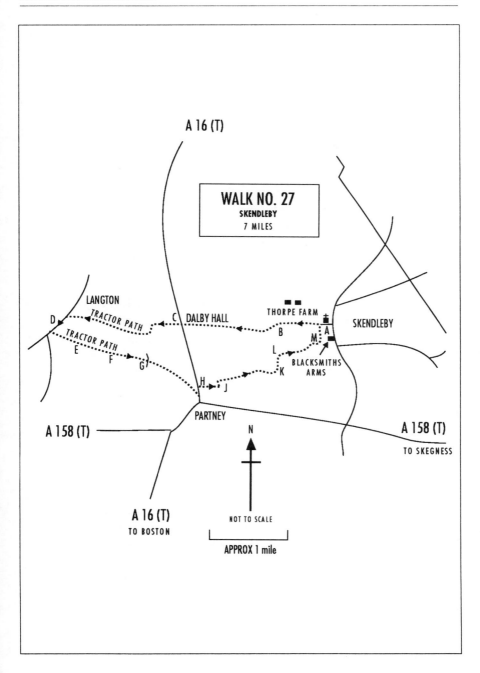

A 16 (T)

WALK NO. 27
SKENDLEBY
7 MILES

LANGTON

D — TRACTOR PATH — C DALBY HALL

THORPE FARM

SKENDLEBY

B

TRACTOR PATH

E   F   G

M   A

L

K   BLACKSMITHS
ARMS

H   J

PARTNEY

N

A 158 (T)

A 158 (T)

TO SKEGNESS

A 16 (T)
TO BOSTON

NOT TO SCALE

APPROX 1 mile

left. The path goes in here and close to the chapel building on your right, so that you will see the path and stile and save yourself the trouble of having to climb the gate to the left.

After a while, about halfway along the route to Partney, there is a derelict building that appears at one time to have been house with stabling, wagon sheds, barn etc (E). Having followed the tractor track for some way, it eventually deserts you at (F) by going left, but the path is still well defined and goes straight ahead. The critical point is at a high stile where a lot of machinery has recently been working (G). A farm track goes across from right to left and might mislead you, but the path is straight ahead, even though it might not be obvious in summer. (Going to the right along the farm road would bring you to a mile of walking on the very busy A158.)

If you feel you should make a small detour because of crops, do it to the left and come back onto the line, aiming again for the tower of the church at Partney. By the time you have gone a quarter mile, the path is obvious and will bring you to Partney by way of the farm road into Grange Farm near the church. From the farm gate, cross the road and walk to the left, then turn right into Madison Lane (H). Walk along the left-hand side of the lane until you are opposite Hudson Close.

There is a path on your left along the edge of the grounds of the primary school (J). Walk along it into the field, turn right at the end of the school and head to the left of a line of hawthorn and the waymark post there. Keep going on that same line, walking at the top of the bank parallel to the stream below on the left. The next stile is already in sight: go across or around the edge of the next field, then over the little stile with its right and left exit. At the next boundary, go up along the right-hand edge to the next stile. Now walk down to a cart track where you turn left (K). The wood will be on your right and at its corner a place where the farmer appears to burn his rubbish. From this corner, go straight across the field, with the edge of the wood from that corner going away at 90 degrees. At the other side, in what is like a little sheltered bay at the right-hand side, is a post at (L) with a circular disc that indicates the path. Start by going down the headland with the hedge on your right, and then about halfway go across the field by bearing slightly left; occasional sighting of Skendleby church will help as the correct line is slightly to the left of the church.

This brings you to a double gate (M) with a stile; once over it you are in the grass field below the church and will join the starting path from the church by turning right.

28. Wainfleet All Saints

Route: Wainfleet All Saints – Friskney Old Fen Bank – Wainfleet All Saints

Pleasant, easy walk in one of the most level parts of Lincolnshire.

Distance:. 6½ miles.

Start: The Market Square (parking is usually possible, but Friday is market day). OS Landranger Series Map 122, square 4958.

Getting there: Follow the A52 from either Skegness or Boston, as the main road goes through the town. There is also a railway station.

The Royal Oak

Like other small market towns that seem to be more like big villages, Wainfleet has a number of friendly comfortable pubs. Consequently you might have to do a bit of personal research for the one that suits you. My own preferences are the Old Chequers Inn and the Royal Oak, favouring the latter. Both are Batemans houses (I have got used to their bitter). The Royal Oak is not too big, is open all day in the late spring and summer, serves food and has accommodation with B&B and evening meals available. I also enjoyed the company of the other customers, which is a good sign.

Beers: Batemans, Guinness and lagers. Open 11am – 11pm most of the year. Any group wanting food or drink during the colder months has only to phone the landlord and he will arrange to be open. Phone: (01754) 880328

Wainfleet All Saints

Coming here from Skegness, Wainfleet All Saints seemed idyllic and calm from the moment of my arrival. As you enter, you pass fine houses and parkland before reaching the Market Square. This was the birthplace of William of Waynflete, first Provost of Eton, Bishop of Winchester, Lord Chancellor and tutor to the Prince of Wales. It was he who obtained the charter to the town, gave Magdalen College to Oxford and in 1484 gave the school of the same name to this town, which has come to be known as the town's finest building. Unfortunately, the church of All Saints was demolished around 1820, but other churches remain. There are two Victorian terraces worth looking at in Barcombe street, and a market cross too. There seem to be some very pleasant people living here too.

The Walk

Starting in the Square (A), make your way down the main road towards the railway level crossing, go over it, and continue along that road and over the bridge that crosses the Steeping River. Now go left (B) and follow the road round as it swings right At the point where the road starts to turn left again, you will see a path on your right (C) into the field or park: walk to the near end of the avenue of trees (D) and then along that avenue.

At the top, turn right and go along the boundary of the sports field until you come to a gate that will allow you through, across the field and to the gap at the other side. This puts you onto a path to follow up to the road. Go over this road, and slightly to your right there is a footpath sign, sometimes hidden by weeds, which points down a path running behind a row of houses.

The reason that this path is not straight, as on the OS map, is that a farmer's objections resulted in the compromise we have today, which at least is reasonably well marked with stiles and bridges in good order. Keep going straight until a tractor path goes to the left. Go with it for about 10 yards, then turn right (E) and head for the left-hand of three trees prominent on the far side of the field. A bridge will be found there, on the left-hand side of the tree, so cross it and go around the boundary to the right straight across if the crop will take it. Either way, you should come out of the field onto a road (F) which goes right to Pepperthorpe Hall (G). This is a nice but isolated house. Take the next turn on the left (H), which is call Hall Gate and passes through Low Grounds: here, it has to be admitted that Lincolnshire is flat in parts. In fact, the spot heights around here are only one, two or three metres. Underfoot the part metalled track turns into a green lane before coming out on the road at the lych gate. Go left to join the road from Friskney and turn right (J), then right again at Old Fen Bank.

A bridge now appears on the left (K). Cross it to walk down the other side of the drain, past a goldfish pond in front of a cottage, a primitive chapel and Chapel Cottage, to the site of an earlier church that fortunately has a concise explanation of what, why and when. Carry on along the same road. After the caravan site, go over the road bridge (L) and Steeping River by Crows Bridge; go right at the first junction and left at the second (M).

If you follow this road and keep going to the right, it will take you over the level crossing, back into Wainfleet All Saints via a small housing development and, just after a road to the left, to the Royal Oak. It is less than 200 yards to the market place.

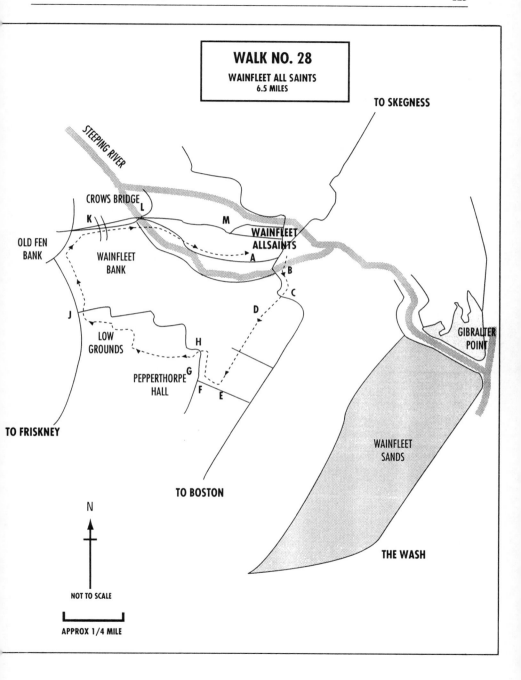

WALK NO. 28

WAINFLEET ALL SAINTS
6.5 MILES

TO SKEGNESS

STEEPING RIVER

CROWS BRIDGE

L

K

M

WAINFLEET
ALLSAINTS

OLD FEN
BANK

WAINFLEET
BANK

A

B

C

D

J

LOW
GROUNDS

H

G

F E

PEPPERTHORPE
HALL

GIBRALTER
POINT

TO FRISKNEY

WAINFLEET
SANDS

TO BOSTON

N

NOT TO SCALE

APPROX 1/4 MILE

THE WASH

29. South Thoresby

Route: South Thoresby – Trout Farm – Belleau – Swaby – South Thoresby.

Short and sweet, finishing along a section of special interest. Some parts may be muddy in poor weather.

Distance: 4 miles.

Start: The Vine Inn (A) or the church (B). OS Landranger Series Map 122, square 4176.

Getting there: From Louth on the A16(T) turn left 3 miles after Burwell. From Alford, turn right off the A1104, 1 mile after passing Alford Hospital.

The Vine

A little gem of a country pub. It has a small hallway/bar (the space behind the bar is surely bigger) but with other small rooms available, there is always some room for the serious business, which here is not so much the beer but the whisky. Any landlord who has over 150 different malt whiskeys, all listed and priced, is not just an enthusiast, he is what makes this Inn special, an expert in a particular part of his trade. Just to talk to him is entertaining, but if you like a a a drop of malt, listen and learn. There is accommodation here, which I should think is quite often considered fortunate, and an excellent breakfast is served.

Beers: with a choice of at least two of Batemans beers, Wards, John Smiths and Tetleys, with an occasional guest beers, this is a `special interest' pub, especially as the walk has something special to offer too. Open all day (even on a Sunday it is open for tea or coffee outside the usual hours). Phone: (01507) 480273

South Thoresby

Like the pub (the present one was built in the eighteenth century) the village has that enduring look, possibly because of well built houses like the Rectory and the quiet that surrounds you as you walk down the lanes. Two small market towns, Alford and Louth are near enough to provide all day-to-day requirements although the nearest Marks and Sparks might be at Grimsby. The only other danger might be from occasional Morris Dancers.

The Walk

Walk past the church at (B) and the unusually high seat placed by the road to commemorate the Silver Jubilee in 1952, to the stile on the left of the gate which has two footpath pointers. Take the one that points to the right and cross the field, going below the high garden wall on your right. Going down to the left after the first boundary, head for a point to the left of the wind pump (C) which can be seen next to what is now the combination of the Swaby Beck and the Calceby Beck. Now go to the stile ahead at the Belleau Trout Farm and turn left for a little way along the road, passing the plantation on the right. At the end of this, turn right and walk up the side of the plantation until you strike off in a straight line away from the far end of the plantation. Any worry you may have at this point is swept away after about 20 paces as it is then, having gained the brow, that Belleau church spire comes into view. Looking to the left of it, the corner of a hedge can be seen. Go to that point and from there, head for the spire. A stile allows you to turn left along the road. On the way you may have noticed not only the view, but also, away to the right, programmed replanting in the woodland. It is very encouraging to see money being reinvested in deciduous trees, especially as it is rather a long term investment.

When you reach the road junction, turn right and look out for a path 5060 yards along on the left at (D), just after the small wood. Go down the field (the path edges to the right, away from the wood) and as you pass the end of the wood, go straight ahead; about 150 yards further on, aim for the two trees at the corner where two hedgerows meet. From there, go left, following the one that will be on your right-hand side. From the corner, go through and as if bisecting the corner, take a line across the field where, most helpfully, there are posts to guide you across. A bit of a spinney is next at the top corner, so go down the side of it until you are in the far corner at the end of the field. Then drop down over the ridge and follow the path through the thicket to the roadside stile (E).

Turn left along the lane to the end, and then walk between the side of the wooden garage on the right and the high hedge on the left (F). This is someone's garden so do take care. The path is well cared for and you will notice a pond above the stream with carp. Following this path brings you to a stile on the right-hand side of the gate; the path goes through a small dale typical of Wold country, except for a healthy stream running along the bottom with a chalk and pebble bed. Most Wolds rivers and streams soaked down into the chalk years ago. That this is chalkland is soon verified as you pass a small landslip on your left, as well as by the many wildflowers that you will see.

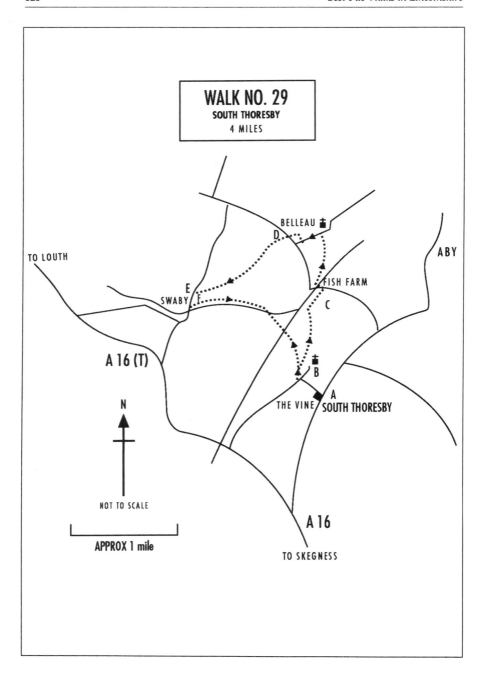

WALK NO. 29
SOUTH THORESBY
4 MILES

TO LOUTH

BELLEAU

ABY

D

E
SWABY F

FISH FARM

C

A 16 (T)

B

THE VINE SOUTH THORESBY

N

NOT TO SCALE

APPROX 1 mile

A 16

TO SKEGNESS

The next section is overgrown with much elderberry, but the path is still clear.

At a sign saying `permissive footpath' there is a map to show where you are, and an alternative route. Our walk goes straight ahead and soon comes to a point where the path splits, going to the left along the field edge and to the right into the wood. Go right, go to the end of the wood, and bear right, noting some big heart-shaped leaves with pink flowers down in the waterside scrub. This is butterburr. Then go down to and over the longish bridge preceded by stepping blocks that mark the old water course, before going to the left over what is frequently a soft to muddy stretch. After a bridge over Calceby Beck swing right along the fence higher up the field. Take the first stile on your right and continue left up to the top of the field, the gate and stile and South Thoresby church. The Vine is just a little further.

The Vine

30. Goxhill

Route: Goxhill – East Marsh Farm – Goxhill Haven – East Halton Skitter – Chapel Farm – South End – Goxhill

Easy, level walking.

Distance: 9 miles.

Start: At the Brocklesby Hunt. Please ask the landlord's permission to park here. If the pub is closed, parking is available just before the church. OS Landranger Series Map 113, square 0921/1021.

Getting there: Approach from the M180 or the Humber Bridge, then the A15(T). Turn left at first roundabout after leaving the Bridge or right at the first roundabout after leaving M180 towards Barton, then on to Barrow on Humber. Go north of the village, and Goxhill is signposted from the next crossroads. The pub is on your right as you approach the level crossing and the car parking space by the church is a little further on, down a lane on the right opposite the shops.

The Brocklesby Hunt

This is a roadside pub that can provide reasonably priced food to go with your drink. The food ranges from a quick snack to a three course meal, all at reasonable prices. There is a large room on the right with pool table etc, but on the left, a pleasant smaller room and bar reveal the landlord's other interest. He is part of an association that keeps alive the memory of and interest in the US Army Airforce fighter training unit that was based at Goxhill airfield, much of which can still be seen. The association formed to this end has erected a small memorial stone and films are shown two evenings a week in the pub. All this is explained and illustrated on the walls of the lounge bar. Such is the enthusiasm of James Chesman that he and Ron Parker run the Goxhill Airfield Tribute, a group of similarly minded people who make sure that we remember that victory in World War II was a shared task. They run guided tours of the airfield, returning to the Brocklesby Hunt for a buffet meal and to watch a video of a film taken by an American airman, with a gun camera taken from a crashed aircraft.

Beers: Cask Stones, Worthington Best Bitter and Bass Mild.Open Monday – Thursday 12am – 3pm, 7 – 11pm; Friday – Saturday 12am – 5pm, 7 – 11pm; usual 10.30pm finish on Sundays. Phone: (01469) 530468

Goxhill

A village of very mixed buildings, including attractive cottages and some elegant houses, clustered around the church. It owes some of its growth and character to the time of the paddleboat ferries and some, no doubt, to the World War II American base. The paddleboat ferries ran from nearby New Holland and were discontinued after the Humber Bridge was built. Regretfully, even the Goxhill Haven is silted up so the commercial connection with the river and the sea is almost lost. The `skitter', named after the next village but almost as near to Goxhill as the haven was, can still provide some shelter and moorings of sorts for the smaller fishing boats.

Other assets are the avenue of trees that you will see if you take a walk around the village to North End; the collection of models and railway memorabilia at the railway station on the Barton Cleethorpes line; and as, mentioned earlier, the illustrated history of the American Army Air Force Fighter Training base.

The Walk

From either the pub or the church (A or B), go to the centre of the village, by the shops, going straight on if you are coming from the Brocklesby Hunt, and turning right if you are coming from the church. Keep going on Main Street so that the cemetery is soon on the right. You will have noticed by now what a neat, well-cared for village this is. The window cleaner, who comes from Immingham to a large number of regulars, told me as we looked across at the old hangars that Clark Gable was stationed here. That failed to excite me.

Go straight across at the crossroads at (C), but not before stopping to take a look at the memorial stone which has a twisted piece of propeller from the Lockheed Lightning featured in the display at the pub.

At the end of Horsegate Field Road, the second part of the road out of the village, you come to a T-junction (D). Turn left. You are surrounded by arable land with very little grass and if it is at all damp, consider wearing wellingtons as this land is very heavy. A duck rearing farm is on the right.

This quiet lane with a good grass verge soon comes to another junction (E); the path is to the right, up to the bank of the River Humber. Don't be tempted to go down the tractor track just before the junction, thinking it might be a short cut; it ends just short of an impassable drain. At the end of the road, before the river bank, there is what seems to be a lonely community. Onto the bank at (F), go right.

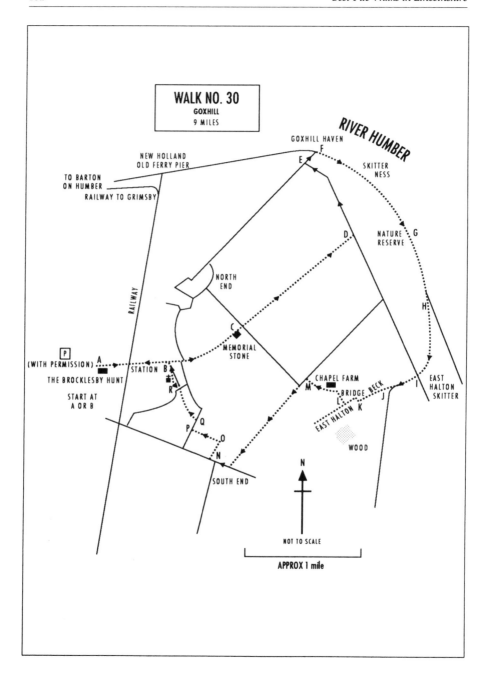

WALK NO. 30
GOXHILL
9 MILES

Walking along this high, wide, protective banking, you can see across the river, two miles wide at this point. On your left are the docks on the east side of Hull and the North Sea ferries terminal. Then you pass Skitter Ness, a point followed by a slight indentation on the bank, and just after that, at (G), the Claypits Nature Reserve on the right. To go into the reserve you need to obtain permission, as numbers are limited at critical times. There are fine views from where you stand over land and river, where there are large numbers of water fowl at certain times. The next prominent marker is the regulating valve station belonging to British Gas and the pipes that seem to come out of the sea.

Only a little further, going down off the bank at (H), East Halton Skitter is on the left. I am told `skitter' means a sheltered anchorage and this one, at (I), seems just big enough for the few small fishing boats tied up there.

The lane comes just after that and you need to go left. If it is a fine day, go up onto the bank on the right. There are often men fishing there and it can be a pleasant place for a sandwich, a coffee or just a sit down.

When you get going up the road, go into the wooded area along the path on the right just where the road turns left (J). It is only a short way along the left-hand side of the beck before you come to a stile. This has a more or less permanent sign saying `bull in field', a common practice in Lincolnshire farming areas 10 years ago. Now it is most unusual. Should there be a bull in the field (it usually has sheep or nothing) it would mean a detour along the road to the Grange, through the farmyard and then the path to the wood, turning sharp right at its corner to get to the brick built bridge (which is marked (K) on the map). If you need to do this, complain to the tourist office who have officially said landowners and councils are doing all they can to encourage walkers. Maybe the sign about the bull is now an antique.

Cross the field by walking alongside the beck, and at the far side go through the gate, turn right, through the next one and over the bridge. Turn left after the bridge and go along the edge of the field, along beside the same beck but on the other side. At some times of year it is difficult to spot the path that goes to the right. To solve such a problem, keep your eye on the square wood, over on the left; walk along the beckside until you can see the bottom boundary and the side that is at first the far side, in equal amounts. They form an arrow pointing towards you. At that point, (L), turn right and walk across the field to a part of the opposite boundary that appears to recede like a little bay in the hedge. You will find two old gateposts when you get there and if the same line of path is continued, you will arrive at the nearest corner of the garden belonging to Chapel Farm. Walk to the left along the edge of the garden until you reach the farm road. Turn left here and follow that road until you reach the road proper (M) to turn left and walk down to South End.

Turn right and go through the village, ignoring the next road on the left and watching out for a path on your right immediately after a modern house with greenhouses and other outbuildings (N). Cross the field with the hedge on your right and go through a gap in the top corner (O). Turn left along a green lane which was once an old railway line. On reaching the road at (P), turn right, and at the next path on the other side of the road (Q), turn left.

Cross two fields, and cross over the lane at the other end to go down the lane opposite at (R), where a short path starting on your left and then going to the right brings you back to the car parking area by the church. If your car is at the pub, go a bit further towards the white house and the shops, turn left onto the main road and walk along to and over the level crossing. Just ahead on the left is the Brocklesby Hunt.

31. Castle Bytham

Route: Castle Bytham – quarries – Pickworth Great Wood – Lime Kiln – Clipsham – Castle Bytham

This walk offers a great variety of scenery on a mildly undulating path.

Distance: 7½ miles.

Start: On the road below the church. OS Landranger Series Map 130, square 9818.

Getting there: Leave the A1 at Stretton and then turn left on leaving Clipsham. Turn left at the next crossroads and Castle Bytham is less than a mile along that road. Street parking is possible.

The Castle Inn

This is very well placed in the centre of the village below the church. It is as pleasant inside as it looks from the outside, with an amiable landlord. Food is served every day, lunchtime and evening.

Beers: Theakstones, Boddingtons and I.P.A. Open 12am – 3pm, but may be earlier on a quiet day, and 7 – 11pm, with the usual Sunday hours. Phone: (01780) 410504

Castle Bytham

Like many a village built on a hillside, it is attractive, but leaves you to wonder if terrace gardening is as arduous as it looks. The stream in the valley runs into the River Glen and on the other side of it are earthworks which are apparently the remains of a Norman castle. Despite the alleged decline of the village after the railway closed, houses are still being built here, and good ones too. Being about 10 miles from Stamford and 15 from Grantham, it seems a very pleasant place to live.

This walk is an `extra' for more than one reason. Although the village is well into Lincolnshire, the walk spends a few miles over the boundary in what was once Rutland, and is set to regain its identity. This is good hunting country. Racehorse trainers have converted the old railway track into training gallops.

The Walk

From the road by the green walk up to the church, then past the old school before going around the left-hand side of the cemetery and through a pair of gates of obvious railway origin. Crossing the bridge, have a look over the side to see the gallop. A future Cheltenham Gold Cup winner might be passing.

Next at (B), go through a field gate and cross the field in front of you, bearing slightly left. It is along this part that you seem to hear the jet engines of Tornadoes taking off from RAF Cottesmore more than elsewhere. This thunderous roar sounds as if they are taking off in bunches.

The path meanwhile goes across the field near its centre and through two gates with stiles. After the second one walk ahead with the hedge on your left-hand side to the far side of the field, coming out onto the road which is crossed at (C). The track opposite goes gradually downhill and except for curves, general points south, aiming for gaps in the hedges and giving you a couple of ditches and a high fence with a low stile, before a right and left turn take you into what might be thought to be just another woodland path. In fact it is not wise to stray more than a few feet from either side of the path; on the right is a deep quarry, now unused, while on the left is an even deeper quarry that is still working. It looks as if its main job at the moment is to hack out giant cubes. The path ends abruptly at a rubbish heap, so turn left and then right where there is a lane running down from the old quarry house.

Cross the road when you come to it and start walking up the marked bridleway, aiming to the right of the hedge that starts a little way in front of you. It will take you alongside the wood for a little way before arriving at the entrance (D) to a well surfaced path that goes right through the centre of Pickworth Wood.

Unfortunately luck does not hold out, as after passing a turning to the left and then one to the right, you are faced with a stretch that goes straight on and is very muddy. It is not a long stretch and it is possible that it dries out occasionally. I hope it has when you arrive.

When you are out of the wood, walk along a drier section of bridleway, that has a slimy green ditch on the right. Soon you are at the farm and then the farm road, at the end of which is the road proper (E). Turn and walk to the right. The hamlet of Pickworth is to the left but unless you are in urgent need of a telephone, there is no real need to visit the place.

More interesting, and a good reason for straying over the border, is the lime kiln that was last used over a hundred years ago. This is on your right, at

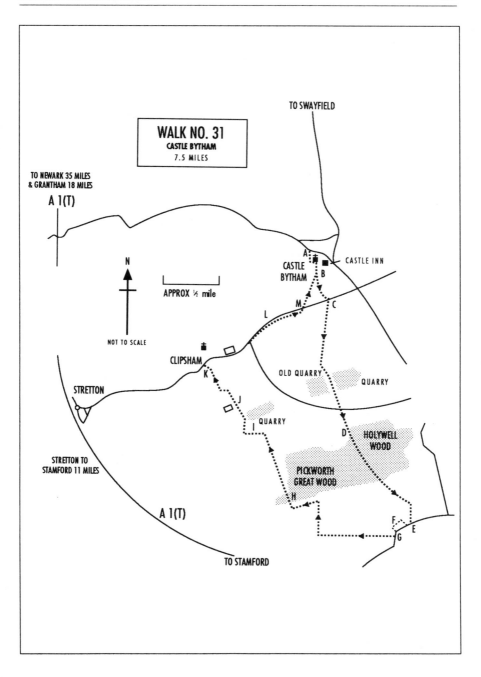

TO SWAYFIELD

WALK NO. 31
CASTLE BYTHAM
7.5 MILES

TO NEWARK 35 MILES
& GRANTHAM 18 MILES

A 1(T)

N

APPROX ½ mile

NOT TO SCALE

A

CASTLE
BYTHAM

CASTLE INN

B

M

C

L

CLIPSHAM

K

OLD QUARRY

QUARRY

STRETTON

J

I

QUARRY

D

HOLYWELL
WOOD

STRETTON TO
STAMFORD 11 MILES

PICKWORTH
GREAT WOOD

H

A 1(T)

F

E

G

TO STAMFORD

(F), just by the village sign, and is worth a stop to absorb the site and read the details that are given on a conveniently placed lectern.

About 100 yards further on, a gateway on the right (G) gives access to another bridleway. Reaching a field boundary with waymarks, look to your right at the wood and then look along it to the left. The path goes to a point near that end, but although the waymark points diagonally across the field to get there, I see no reason why you should not go round the edges of the field. This way, the walking is easier and as you go along the edge of the wood which has a bluebell-decorated edge in April you cannot miss the path that goes through the thin bit of the wood, marked (H).

Coming out at the other side, look down the edge of the wood that runs away from you and aim off to the left by about 12 degrees. On your way across this field, your might notice a couple of high seats. They are like giant tennis umpires' chairs with the seat about 10 feet off the ground. I noticed that they were well secured but I am still wondering what they are used for. The path eventually (it's a big field) brings you to a small triangular wood. Go round the left-hand side of it and then resume the previous line. Another quarry is passed, way over on your right and by then you will be on a more obvious track. This track goes up to a couple of walls that are all that remain of an old farm building (J). Take the path to the right of it, which goes down by the side of the wood; I saw six deer come crashing out from here to cross the field in front.

At the bottom, cross the stream by the stout bridge and walk all the way up the field before going through a gate, and then diagonally left to the far left corner of the smaller paddock and also to the left of a small dew pond. There is the short lane that takes you to the road at (K).

Here is the place to turn right around the next corner where the Olive Branch, Clipsham's pub, stands, advertising its real ales and food. The village with its pleasing mixture of type and size of building makes you wonder what the planners of today would have made of it in their demand for uniformity.

Now continue along the road, where after a mile you will come to an astonishing collection of clipped yews (L). First you see what appear to be giant chessmen around a small gatehouse, but as you walk further, there is a drive almost half a mile long lined with more of them. Topiary no longer seems all that attractive to me, Clipsham Hall or not.

After another half or three-quarters of a mile there is first a white cottage with stables or barn on the left. At (M) and before the next cottage, take the path indicated by going through the gate and following the hedge on your right. Climb over the next stile, go left and aim to the left of a small clump of hawthorn before going for the gateway you can now see on the far side of the field. Climb the stile at the side of the gate and start to walk towards the two pine trees ahead of you. The path will now be recognisable as the first part of the start, so it only remains to cross the railway bridge again and go down past the church and you will come out at the green and outside the Castle Inn.

Topiary near Clipsham Hall: beauty in the eye of the beholder

The Sigma Leisure Pub Walks series includes:

Cheshire

Derbyshire

Glasgow

Leeds

The Lake District (central area)

The Lake District (fringes)

Lancashire

Northumbria

Nottinghamshire

The Peak District

Sheffield

Shropshire

Snowdonia

Tyneside

Yorkshire Dales

Each book costs £6.95 and contains an average of 25 excellent walks: far better value than any other competitor!

SIGMA LEISURE, 1 SOUTH OAK LANE, WILMSLOW, CHESHIRE SK9 6AR.
Phone: 01625-531035; Fax: 01625-536800.
E-mail: info@sigmapress.co.uk
Web site: http//www.sigmapress.co.uk

VISA and MASTERCARD orders welcome.